The Art Of FORGIVENESS

The Art Of FORGIVENESS

A Practical Guide for Self-Healing and Overcoming Past Traumas

BY

KURT GASSNER

The Art Of Forgiveness
Kurt Gassner

First Edition, 2022

Impressum
My-mindguide – The publishing trademarke of trendguide Capital GmbH, Klenzestr. 42a, 80469 Munich, Germany.

Reg. Nr. HRB Munich 206639, VAT 152 123 159, CEO: Kurt Friedrich Gassner
Web: www.my-mindguide.com, mail: gassner@my-mindguide.com

Paperback ISBN: 978-3-949978-09-8
Ebook ISBN: 978-3-949978-10-4
Hardback ISBN:978-3-949978-11-1

Contents

Chapter 1

THE ART OF FORGIVENESS

While forgiveness is far easier to discuss than truly deliver, there do exist techniques that will make the process easier. It is frequently stated that you cannot force someone to forgive you. What is less frequently stated is that you cannot make someone forgive you. Forgiveness is a process and one that is frequently elusive. We've all had someone do us wrong.

Occasionally, an apology goes a great way toward alleviating our anger and hurt. Sometimes, we might find happiness in the legal system when justice prevails. At other times, our outrage over crimes committed against us is increased by the absence of an apology or a failure of legal justice, making forgiveness that much more difficult to accomplish.

Shakespeare imparted this timeless insight: "It is in pardoning that we are pardoned," which echoes an even older idiom found in the Lord's Prayer: "Forgive us our sins, as we forgive those who trespass against us."

Another astute discourse on forgiveness that has stayed with me came from an underrated intelligent woman, the late Tammy

Faye Baker, the ex-wife of scandal-plagued evangelist Jim Baker. Tammy Faye was a woman who suffered tremendously at the hands of her ex-husband, her congregation, the press, and the public. In a biographical documentary titled *The Eyes of Tammy Faye*, she discusses forgiveness and the damage that the lack thereof can cause. In her own peculiar, poetic way, Baker explains that harboring a grudge is akin to lugging around a heavy dead body swarming with maggots. It's not harmful to the person at whom the resentment is aimed; rather, it infects and sickens the one who bears this burden.

The majority of informed sources, from spiritual leaders to philosophers and psychotherapists, believe that harboring ill will against another generates discontent in the owner of those feelings. However, few of these professionals can offer guidance on truly forgiving. Some individuals erroneously believe that they must simply give up their hateful sentiments. This saying brings to mind another: "Easier said than done."

When people learn that I've been scammed out of money or that I've had my home burglarized numerous times or that others have tried to take what is legally mine, they often wonder how I've managed to stay upright in the end.

As the alternative to forgiving these wrongs is resentment or a breakdown, I've had to find ways to maintain my sanity and continue living and thriving in life; therefore, I offer these recommendations to people who have been mistreated and abused to set the wheels of forgiveness in action.

Put yourself in the wrongdoer's shoes. Most likely, the individual has a history of being mistreated and lied to, or they may or may not have some physiological disease that contributes to their downward spiral. On the one hand, love, honesty, and kindness come from a pure heart; on the other hand, hatred, deception, and evil originate from a dark and broken heart. Try to empathize with the evildoer and their illness; while this doesn't make their actions ethical, it alleviates the sense that their actions were intended for you.

Concentrate on yourself. Focus on the positive aspects of forgiving for yourself instead of imagining the whole process is for your offender's sake if you can't bear the thought of extending forgiveness to them. Otherwise, you're still letting them win the battle. Don't allow darkness to dominate light. Continue on a larger path of self-development. Demonstrate to the person who deceived you that you are stronger than their negative powers. Make retribution truly sweet in this instance. Your reward will be a happy existence.

Consider moving forward and upward. If you cannot forget and move on from the pain inflicted on you, make an effort to gaze forward rather than backward. Redirect your anger's energy toward a new purpose. Pursue an unfulfilled passion or aspiration—even a tiny one, such as learning a new skill, mastering new technology, taking up a new activity, or volunteering your time in supporting a worthwhile cause. The diversion will benefit you, and you may discover a new source of happiness, connection, or even prosperity, all the while benefitting others.

Recognize a lesson. Consider your negative experience as a good education in the field where the offense occurred if a business partner has duped you; extract whatever lessons you can about how you got yourself into a precarious position. Be mindful of and apply these lessons to your future undertakings.

Similarly, if you ignored red flags, endured unpleasant behavior, or set yourself up for this situation to occur in a relationship, take notice. Don't allow this to ever happen again. Proactively avoid becoming a victim in the future, or end the relationship before you become a victim again. Consider treachery a service that will assist you in avoiding a more costly emotional or financial error in the future.

Assume accountability. All of us are ultimately responsible for our activities and choices. Whatever position you find yourself in, whomever you decided to associate with, and whatever choices you made to reach that point, you put yourself there and made those choices on your own, unless someone held a gun to your head. Recognizing that you made the choices allows you to reclaim control. However, rather than being angry at yourself or distraught up perceived errors, recognize that you do have control. This recognition is powerful and bound to assist you in the future.

Victim
Perpetrator

Chapter 2

WHAT IS THE DEFINITION OF FORGIVENESS?

I've been teaching forgiveness for almost a decade, and the basic explanation I use now is that forgiveness is the capacity to accept the word "no."

People have come to me with various issues, and the common thread running through them all is: I didn't get what I wanted. I received a "no." I desired faithfulness from my relationship; they lacked it. I received a "no." I desired that someone tell the truth; instead, they spoke a falsehood. I received a "no." As a child, I desired to be loved; but, I wasn't cherished in a way that made me feel good. I received a "no."

It's critical to comprehend the common experience—namely, disagreeing with the way life is and attempting to substitute your desired alternative, then being frustrated when it doesn't work.

The core of forgiveness is resilience in the face of setbacks—to be at peace with "no," to be at peace with what is, to be at peace with the fundamental frailty of human life. Then you must proceed and live your life free of prejudice.

The absence informs forgiveness of prejudice. You realize that nobody owes you anything—that you aren't obligated to accept the pain you have endured and pass it on to someone else. Simply because your previous partner was unkind to you doesn't mean you must always extend the third degree to your new companion. You move on with an open heart and accept without prejudice.

You accept it not because life is awful and there's nothing you can do about it—though that may, at times, be true—but because you accept it in a way that allows you to give the next moment a chance.

The Resolution of Grief

However, before one can forgive, one must grieve.

At its most fundamental level, forgiveness is synonymous with grief. As I understand it now, the normal response to being offended, hurt, or assaulted is to grieve. These issues can be viewed as losses—of emotion, a human being, or a dream—and when we lose anything, human beings go through a natural reintegration process known as mourning. Then, forgiveness is how grief is resolved.

However, the difficulties we face with mourning are twofold: Some people never grieve, while others grieve for an excessive amount of time.

A true human being feels pain and accepts suffering as a natural part of the human experience. Without acknowledging that you have been wounded and have lost something, you'll miss out on the benefits of the experience—not only of identifying your pain and mistreatment but also of healing. As a result, there is a strength that comes from experience.

However, a profound human being also lets go of their suffering—they don't preserve it indefinitely, don't build their personality around it, and don't use it as a weapon. Never cling to the unpleasant aspects of an experience to hold yourself accountable for your failings.

Per my observations, three stages of grief must be completed before a person can begin to feel forgiven by another.

The Forgiveness Process

The first stage is to completely identify the pain caused, whether by you or someone else, and to accept that you've lost something—that you didn't obtain something you desired and it hurts. This may entail difficult work in a therapeutic setting. Sometimes, it takes therapeutic work to convince someone to forgive because they've buried or denied a negative experience, and it may require more effort to convince them to realize the pain or its effects.

This is the second stage of the mourning process, which involves experiencing feelings generally associated with the terrible event itself. It is insufficient for someone to simply state, "Hey, I was beaten for twelve years, and I want to get over it," if they have never been open about their feelings before. They're going to have to suffer to relinquish it. I've never met somebody who didn't suffer on some level due to actual loss. You're feeling various emotions—you're sad and you're afraid. However, when you forgive, you recognize alternatives to prolonged suffering. You're not relinquishing control of the event—that's unchangeable. However, you can alter your emotional response to it.

The third and last phase is rooted in another fundamental truth: the nature of your grief cannot be concealed. I try not to forgive people for things they haven't shared with others because there is so much data on resilience that shows that people who have negative experiences but don't tell anyone have significantly worse outcomes than those who do share. The human connection is critical in the healing process.

That being said, those who broadcast their grievance to the entire world have the second-worst outcomes. Resilience research demonstrates that sharing your concern with a few select, caring people over time is necessary for a healthy reaction to difficulty. You don't divulge your innermost thoughts to anyone, and you don't divulge your innermost thoughts. I've recommended that those without trusted confidants see a therapist or enroll in a twelve-step program—anything to ensure they're not harboring any shame.

If you follow these stages, you can arrive at a point in your grieving where you are willing to forgive. However, it takes time. A mother once told me, "I need to forgive someone for murdering my kid," at one of my early workshops on forgiveness.

I was at a loss for words. Because I hadn't previously worked with relatives of murder victims, the only question I could ask was, "When did it happen?"

"A month ago," she said.

"Go home," I told her. This isn't what you require at the moment. Return in two years. Return once you've endured the unfathomably difficult task of grieving that loss, and then try your best to forgive."

How to Overcome Forgiveness Obstacles

It's difficult to let go of the pain produced by another's misbehavior. Is there anything that prevents us from forgiving others?

When Laurie and Jamie came to my office a few months ago, they were stuck in the typical stalemate that often occurs during couples' therapy. Laurie learned the previous week that Jamie had committed the almost unforgivable: he had had a brief romance with his new administrative assistant when Laure was out of town visiting her dying father. Jamie was sincere in his repentance, but he also had a grudge against Laurie for repeatedly exceeding their agreed-upon limit on their credit card, despite his several efforts to stay within their agreed-upon budget.

We are all aware of such consequences—how being wounded, betrayed, or abused can harden into long-lasting grudges or resentments. I've spent the last two decades assisting couples like Laurie and Jamie in regaining their feeling of trust following a breach of their vows or commitment. During that period, I've discovered that it's critical to assist people to understand one another's underlying motivations to mend a rift.

However, I've learned that assisting individuals in forgiving one another is critical, especially when legitimate reasons to resist are present. Indeed, study after study indicates that our inability to forgive past wrongs can negatively affect our mental and physical health.

Forgiveness is the act of releasing oneself from the pain created by the transgression. This doesn't imply ignoring, disregarding, forgetting, condoning, trivializing the injury, or rushing to a premature or shallow reconciliation; in fact, reconciliation isn't always necessary. Rather, it entails altering our relationship via comprehension, compassion, and release. Forgiveness' emotional, bodily, and social advantages have been repeatedly established over decades of social psychology studies. Genuine forgiveness mends broken relationships and provides inner peace.

Nonetheless, we frequently struggle to let go, forgive, and move on. Research indicates that we might remain trapped in fear or hostility for days, months, or even years, even when we feel compassion and empathy for the person who has wounded us.

Why is it so tough for us to do something helpful to our well-being? That's the question Ian Williamson of New Mexico Highlands University and Marti Gonzales of the University of Minnesota have investigated through their research on psychological barriers to forgiveness.

Williamson, Gonzales, and colleagues define three main forms of "forgiveness aversion" in a recent study published in *Motivation and Emotion*. Historically, views about assisting another person in forgiving another person have included either increasing one's empathy or compassion for the perpetrator or "distancing," or not taking things personally. However, their research on forgiveness aversion offers another approach: Forgiveness occurs when the victim's anxieties and concerns are addressed, not by appealing to kindness or compassion. Williamson and Gonzales' research recommends strategies for coping with perceived barriers to forgiveness and moving toward forgiveness safely and authentically.

I provide a brief overview of the three hurdles to forgiveness and strategies for overcoming them, based on research and my therapeutic experience with hundreds of couples and people. Understanding these obstacles to forgiveness can be extremely beneficial for clinicians and anyone who has ever battled with forgiveness—which is to say, the vast majority of us.

Barrier #1: Unreadiness

The first impediment is "unreadiness," which Williamson and Gonzales define as an internal condition of unresolved emotional distress that can impede or derail forgiveness. Individuals may become trapped in a victim cycle, ruminating on the wrongs committed against them by another person or by life itself, leaving them unable to shift their perspective—unable to see the meaning, purpose, lessons, and opportunities for transformation inherent to the occurrences.

Who is most at risk of experiencing unpreparedness? Williamson and Gonzales discovered that individuals' propensity for anxiety and meditating on the gravity of the offending behavior reliably predicted an inability to forgive. Individuals demonstrated a greater unwillingness to move toward forgiveness, particularly when they harbored a fear of repeated offense. How can we overcome this barrier of unreadiness? Williamson and Gonzales' research reaffirms the common belief that "time cures all wounds" and emphasizes the critical importance of not speeding the process of forgiveness. Certainly, time helps people separate themselves from immediate hurt, uncertainty, and rage; it enables the offender to develop a track record of new trustworthy behavior. It enables the victim to reframe the seriousness of the injury from the perspective of the entire relationship.

I witnessed Laurie and Jamie fight and ultimately overcome the obstacle of unreadiness over the three months I worked with them. Laurie was able to contextualize Jamie's transgression within the context of a seventeen-year marriage that had already withstood far more difficult circumstances than Jamie's one night of out-of-bounds activity. And, when Laurie's spending habits improved over time, Jamie could lessen his supervision and stress.

Tips to Overcome Unreadiness

1. Recall the instance of transgression you are unable to forgive. "Light up the networks" of this experience by recalling a visual image, observing the emotions that surface as you recollect this event, and observing the locations in your body where you feel those feelings as contraction, heaviness, or churning. Take note of your own and the other person's thinking when you trigger this memory. Allow this moment to permeate your awareness.

2. Consider the possible lessons of this moment: what could you have done differently? Can you think of anything the other side could've done differently? What would you do differently in the future? When we can transform a regrettable situation into an educational opportunity and even locate the gift in error, we might reopen our perspectives to the possibility of transformation and forgiveness.

Barrier #2: Self-Protection

The second impediment to forgiveness is "self-protection"—a worry, which is frequently justified, that forgiveness may backfire and expose the person providing forgiveness to additional damage, aggressiveness, boundary violations, exploitation, or abuse.

Who is most prone to self-protection? According to Williamson and Gonzales' research, individuals who have repeatedly encountered harmful behavior without receiving an apology are most likely to resist forgiving the offending party. Indeed, they discovered that even the most compelling reason to forgive—the desire to continue a close relationship—can be diminished by the perceived seriousness of the transgression and a perceived lack of true apology or sorrow. Refusing to forgive is an attempt to rebalance the relationship's power or influence.

According to their study, one of the most difficult judgments people ever have to make about forgiveness is this: Can I meet my fundamental needs in this relationship? Or do I need to end this relationship to meet my basic needs, which include safety and trust? The offender's continued behavior is critical in this case. The continuation of the hurtful behavior; the denial or minimization of any sense of wrongdoing; the continued diminution of the recipient's sense of self by another; the continued breakdown of trust; the continuation of the victim's sense of self; the continuation of the victim's sense of self-being blamed for the offender's behavior: the continuation of any or all of these factors can make forgiveness feel impossible, if not foolish.

How can we breach the self-protective barrier? "Victims may reasonably fear that forgiveness exposes them to additional abuse," the researchers write. "Interestingly, when people feel themselves to be more powerful in a relationship, they are more likely to forgive, maybe because they have fewer self-protective concerns in their relationships with their offenders."

In other words, people occasionally have understandable anxieties that extending forgiveness may be (mis)interpreted by the offender as an indication that they can continue to commit the same act. Frequently, individuals must understand that they have the right to establish and enforce legitimate limits in a partnership. Forgiveness might also entail ceasing contact with the offender or altering the norms and power dynamics that govern the relationship's continuation.

Jamie could relinquish his need for self-protection and offer true forgiveness for Laurie's past crimes only after Laurie ceased her excessive spending and began to respect Jamie's monthly budget constraints. When Laurie regained trust in Jamie's sincerity and repentance for his betrayal and in the fact that the conduct would never occur again, she was able to let go of her need for self-protection and forgive.

How to Set Limits

1. Identify one boundary you've been hesitant to establish with the individual you seek to extend forgiveness.
2. Convince yourself that establishing this restriction represents and supports your values, interests, and desires. Consider your comprehension of the other person's values and desires. Take note of any areas of agreement between the two of you; take note of any areas of disagreement.
3. Initiate a discussion with the other person regarding boundaries. Begin by expressing gratitude for their time

spent listening to you. Declare the subject; articulate your comprehension of your own and their requirements.

4. State your boundary simply, plainly, and unequivocally. You have already articulated the principles, requirements, and wants that motivate the restriction; you aren't required to justify, explain, or defend your stance. Indicate the ramifications for the partnership if this limit isn't adhered to.

5. Agree with the other party on the behaviors they can perform and when they can perform them to indicate that they understand your boundary, its necessity, and its benefit.

6. After the allotted "test" period, discuss the changes in the connection, whether the limit was observed, and the next step in enforcing the limit. Changing the dynamics of your relationship may require a few repetitions of this activity.

Barrier #3: "Face" Concerns

The third obstacle is "face" concerns—what we may refer to as the need to maintain one's public reputation and prevent challenges to one's own self-concept—i.e., the sense that "I'm a pushover" or "I'm a doormat."

As social beings, we are hardwired to avoid appearing weak, fragile, or pitiful in front of others. We will defend ourselves against feelings of inner guilt in various ways, and one of them may be a reluctance to forgive. Additionally, researchers discovered that harboring a grudge might provide people with a sense of control over their connections; they may think that forgiving will rob them of this "social authority." Suppose our concerns about preserving our face lead us to crave retaliation or retribution rather than forgiveness. In that case, we may need to rebuild our internal sense of self-worth and self-respect before forgiveness becomes an option.

Who is most prone to have facial concerns? The fear of losing control, concern over social standing, or even a desire for retribution may prevent people from forgiving because they believe the transgression has diminished their self-worth. "To the degree that victims fear seeming weak by forgiving, and are concerned with portraying an image of authority and interpersonal control," the researchers write, "they should be more averse to the prospect of forgiving."

How can we overcome the stumbling block posed by face concerns? Frequently, those who have harmed must reclaim their sense of self-respect and self-worth to create the mental space in which forgiveness appears to be a viable option. We must cultivate and sustain an internal subjective reality—a sense of self—that is unaffected by unfavorable views and expectations. Good friends, trusted family members, therapists, and clergy can all be extremely beneficial in serving as a true other to one's true self—figures who can generate a more positive sense of self.

Laurie and Jamie kept their troubles from friends and family, so they didn't have to worry about their social reputations. They did, however, need to overcome the shame-blaming habits that were prominent when they initially entered couples' counseling. They needed to focus on not taking things personally and on reestablishing mutual appreciation and worthiness before they could move toward forgiveness.

Giving forgiveness is a difficult thing to accomplish. Sincere intentions and consistent practice, over time, is required. However, overcoming reluctance, if not outright unwillingness, can be facilitated by understanding these specific aversions to forgiveness and properly addressing the respective hurdles.

Improving Your Perception of Yourself

1. Take a comfortable seat, and let your eyes softly close. Concentrate on your breathing.

2. When you're ready, recall someone in your life who makes you feel secure. This someone might be a close friend, a therapist, a teacher, a spiritual figure, or even your own wiser self.

3. Visualize yourself sitting face to face with this individual. Consider the person's acceptance, kindness, admiration, and happiness when they gaze at you. Consider how you are absorbing their love and acceptance of you.

4. Now envision yourself as the other person, seeing into your own eyes. Sensitize yourself to the person's love and openness. Consider the kindness that the other person sees in you. Take pleasure in your realization of your goodness.

5. Now revert to your natural state. You are back in your own body, enjoying the other person's gaze with tenderness and compassion. When someone loves and accepts you, you may experience a variety of physical sensations in your body, including a warm feeling in the pit of your stomach.

6. Pause for a moment to consider your experience. You're regaining a favorable image of yourself. Make a conscious effort to recall this sensation as necessary.

Helper
Perpetrator
Victim

Chapter 3

TAKING THE STEPS TO SELF-FORGIVENESS

Forgiveness is frequently defined as a conscious decision to let go of sentiments of wrath, resentment, and retaliation toward someone who has harmed you. While you may be quite forgiving toward others, you may be a lot tougher on yourself.

While everyone makes blunders, developing the ability to learn from them, let go, move on, and forgive yourself is critical for mental health and well-being. Learning more about why self-forgiveness can be useful, shedding light on how to improve your ability to forgive your own faults.

How to Compassionately Forgive Yourself

Self-forgiveness is neither a way of absolving oneself of responsibility nor a sign of weakness. Whatever the circumstances, forgiveness doesn't mean that you condone the actions of those who have harmed you in the past.

Forgiveness entails accepting the action, accepting what occurred, and being willing to go on with your life without dwelling on previous occurrences that cannot be altered. According to one therapeutic approach to self-forgiveness, four fundamental behaviors may be beneficial.

The 4 R's of Self-Forgiveness

1. Responsibility
2. Remorse
3. Restoration
4. Renewal

Accept Responsibility

Self-forgiveness entails more than simply putting the past behind you and moving on. It's about accepting what has occurred and practicing self-compassion.

Confronting your actions or past events is the first step toward self-forgiveness. This is additionally the most troublesome stage. In the event that you've been rationalizing, supporting, or legitimizing your demonstrations, hoping to make them appear OK, it's an ideal opportunity to take ownership of your activities and acknowledge liability.

By accepting responsibility for your acts that have caused harm to others, you can avoid negative emotions such as excessive regret and guilt.

Express Remorse

You may experience several negative emotions resulting from accepting responsibility, including guilt and humiliation. When you've done something wrong, it's perfectly natural and even beneficial to feel guilty. Guilt and remorse can act as a catalyst for constructive behavioral change.

While guilt implies that you are a nice person who did something wrong, shame forces you to view yourself negatively. This may elicit emotions of worthlessness, which, if left unresolved, may manifest in addiction, depression, or aggressiveness. Recognize that committing mistakes that you feel terrible about doesn't automatically make you a bad person or diminish your essential worth.

Repair the Damage and Restore Trust

Making apologies is a critical component of forgiveness, especially when the forgiver is oneself. Just as you may not forgive somebody until they make amends in some way, forgiveness for yourself is more likely to "stick" if you feel as though you have earned it.

One strategy for overcoming your guilt is to take action to correct your errors. Apologize if necessary and seek out ways to make amends to those you have wronged.

While it may appear as though this stage of the process is just for the benefit of the person you've injured, there is something in it for you as well. Correcting your error eliminates the possibility of ever wondering if you could have done more.

Focus on Renewal

Everybody makes errors for which they feel guilty. Rumination, self-hatred, or even pity can be detrimental and make it more difficult to retain self-esteem and motivation.

Forgiving yourself frequently entails identifying a means to grow personally due to the experience. To accomplish this, you must first comprehend why you behaved in the way you did and why you feel bad. What steps can you take now to keep yourself from falling back into the same bad behaviors in the future? Even though you committed a blunder, you learned from the experience and can use it to make better decisions in the future.

Limitations

While self-forgiveness is a potent practice, it's critical to understand that this approach isn't intended for those who unjustly blame themselves for something they're not responsible for.

Individuals who have experienced abuse, trauma, or loss, for example, may experience shame and guilt despite their lack of control. This is especially true when individuals believe they should have been able to forecast and hence avert a poor outcome (an example of what is known as the hindsight bias).

Benefits

The psychology hypothesis has long been that forgiving is a good thing that comes with several benefits, regardless of whether you have suffered a tiny slight or a far more substantial grievance. This means forgiving both others and oneself.

Mental Illness

Letting go and forgiving yourself can help raise your sense of well-being and improve your self-image. Numerous studies have shown that when individuals practice self-forgiveness, their levels of despair and anxiety decrease. On the other hand, self-compassion is related to increased levels of success, productivity, focus, and concentration.

Physical Fitness

Forgiveness can also have a beneficial effect on your physical health. According to a study, you can minimize your chance of a heart attack and improve your cholesterol levels by forgiving those who have hurt you.

Relationships

Self-compassion and forgiveness are also key components of healthy relationships.

While the ability to form strong emotional relationships with others is critical, so can mend those bonds when they become strained or damaged.

According to one study, both parties benefit when the "offending partner" demonstrates self-forgiveness. As a result of real self-forgiveness, both couples reported increased relationship satisfaction and fewer negative thoughts about the other.

Challenges

So, what is it about self-forgiveness that makes it so tough at times? Why do individuals frequently continue to blame and criticize themselves for seemingly minor errors? Engaging in behaviors that contradict our values or self-beliefs can result in feelings of shame and regret—or, in the worst-case scenario, self-loathing.

Certain individuals are simply more prone to ruminating than others, which might make it easier to dwell on negative emotions. Self-forgiveness is made more difficult because it requires confessing fault and accepting that you may need to change.

Finally, those who aren't yet ready to change may have difficulty fully forgiving themselves. Rather than recognizing they may need to change, individuals may participate in self-forgiveness by ignoring or justifying their actions.

Potential Drawbacks

While self-forgiveness is typically regarded as a beneficial activity that can aid in the restoration of one's sense of self, research indicates that it can occasionally have a harmful effect. The primary disadvantage of self-forgiveness is that it can occasionally erode empathy for people harmed by your acts.

While self-forgiveness frequently alleviates guilt, this inner emphasis may make it more difficult to identify with others. This can be avoided by intentionally empathizing with individuals impacted by your actions.

While forgiving others by whom you've been wronged, you can "toughen up," as forgiving oneself can be just as difficult. It's critical to realize that self-forgiveness isn't a one-size-fits-all procedure.

It's never simple or quick, but cultivating this type of self-compassion may result in various health benefits.

Along with reducing stress, despair, and anxiety, self-forgiveness has improved physical health and interpersonal connections.

Seven Techniques for Self-Forgiveness

Forgiveness can be difficult. When someone causes you pain, it can be difficult to let go and go on. Although forgiving others can be difficult at times, forgiving others is frequently far easier than forgiving oneself. Everybody makes errors. Perhaps you missed your daughter's game-winning goal because you arrived late for work, told a falsehood that caused difficulties for others, or your actions had life-altering repercussions. Self-forgiveness enables significant growth, substantial change, and increased emotional well-being regardless of what occurred. Ahead are seven suggestions for practicing self-forgiveness.

Justifications for Self-Forgiveness

Concentrating on unpleasant feelings such as guilt, wrath, or humiliation can negatively affect your mental and physical health. Ruminating on these emotions maintains a state of alertness in your nervous system. In response to these emotions, adrenaline release can result in cardiovascular problems, autoimmune illnesses, and mental health problems such as anxiety and depression. Beating yourself repeatedly increases feelings of guilt and humiliation and the resulting self-belief of being a nasty person. Stuck in the past, you cannot move forward and gain critical lessons. Self-forgiveness permits you to disentangle your identity from your faults. In this manner, you can begin to understand the consequences of your actions and seek opportunities to make amends when possible. It will be easier to forgive others fully when you begin to forgive yourself. Forgiveness is a gradual process. The following are some guidelines to get you started on your path to self-forgiveness and acceptance.

1. Establish a Definition for Forgiveness

Having a firm grasp of forgiveness and what it means to you is a critical first step. Your definition may be influenced by your religious beliefs, family history, or personal values. When defining forgiveness, be certain to include a definition of what it *isn't*. Though you may believe that forgiveness absolves you of responsibility or implies that you are blameless, you'll remain trapped in shame and/or denial by viewing forgiveness as a process of forgetting or moving on as if nothing happened. This is why a precise definition of forgiveness is critical. Perhaps forgiveness can be described as accepting one's flaws. However, rather than continuing to punish yourself and wallow in humiliation, you have chosen to treat yourself with compassion and understanding to learn from this experience, accept responsibility for your actions, and grow in ways that promote meaningful transformation.

2. Recognize Your Emotions

To forgive oneself, you must acknowledge, not reject, your feelings. Make time to reflect on your sentiments without passing judgment. Identify your feelings and allow yourself to feel them. You can feel anything you need to feel, and your reactions don't have to be defined by these feelings. This may be challenging, but you won't be able to let go of your feelings of guilt and shame unless you accept, feel, and work through them. It's natural to feel regret if you have caused another person suffering. Recognizing these emotions assists you in acquiring a complete understanding of what happened. Ignoring your feelings might result in more regret, making self-forgiveness extremely difficult.

3. Acknowledge Your Actions

You cannot truly learn from your mistakes until you can admit them. Recognize what occurred and accept responsibility for your role in it to understand why you acted the way you did. Put your judgment aside and consider the facts of the situation and your role in it. When you learn the lessons associated with your actions, you may also take steps to avoid repeating them. Living in denial prevents you from owning up to and learning from your mistakes. Similarly, repeating the situation repeatedly focuses on what went wrong rather than on what you learned. If you can identify the behaviors and activities that contribute to the problem, you can take the required steps to impact change.

4. Express Regret

Apologize if your actions caused someone else damage. A sincere apology to someone you've wronged might go a long way toward achieving self-forgiveness. It will likely be tough to truly forgive yourself if you still feel the need to make amends to another person. While you can't know how someone will react to your apology, you can let go of the circumstance and find forgiveness for yourself by apologizing to the offended party. If you have caused another person harm and cannot apologize, writing down what you wish to say can help you avoid obsessing about it. You may also write an apology to yourself. To appear sincere in your apology, you must own your wrongdoing, explain why you regret it, acknowledge the hurt you have caused, and detail what you want to do differently in the future to guarantee it doesn't happen again.

5. Concentrate on What You've Learned

Important lessons are far simpler to learn when things go wrong than right. If you can focus on the learning experience and what you will do better in the future, self-forgiveness may become more acceptable. When you understand what you did and the ramifications, you can make a different option in the future. Sometimes the most efficient way to learn this lesson is to make a mistake. What went wrong is understandable, but nothing will change if this is your only source of knowledge. By concentrating on the adjustments that need to be made in the future, you can learn from the experience. When you regard it as a difficult lesson learned, you may find it easier to forgive yourself.

6. Make Significant Changes

Changing your behavior may be necessary before you can forgive yourself. Recognizing that your behaviors contributed to the problem is merely the first step. Additionally, you must alter your conduct. If you continue to engage in problematic behavior, you absolve yourself of responsibility for your actions. Through behavioral modification, it's possible to attain a more favorable outcome. For instance, if you're constantly late for work and feel horrible about it, you can improve your performance by leaving the house early. If changing your conduct wouldn't improve the situation, you can still make a significant improvement in another way. You may volunteer, tell your story, or strive to create a future solution. Paying it forward is an excellent method to refocus your attention away from what you did wrong and onto what you are doing to correct it.

7. Show Compassion

Just as you can demonstrate compassion toward others, you can demonstrate compassion toward yourself. Constantly criticizing oneself for something that has already occurred and cannot be reversed promotes damaging negativity. This can result in a distressing self-perception of yourself as a broken person unworthy of grace. Instead, you might show yourself kindness and acceptance. Communicate with oneself in the same manner you would with a friend. Recognize that making an error doesn't automatically make *you* a mistake. While you're probably more critical of yourself than anybody else, how you treat yourself is a choice. Compassionate and understanding treatment of oneself can assist you in practicing forgiveness for both yourself and others.

While forgiving yourself may be difficult, it's critical for your mental well-being. Individual counseling may be beneficial if you have difficulty forgiving yourself for past transgressions. You don't have to forget what happened to forgive yourself, so keep that in mind. When you forgive yourself, you can experience significant development and change, benefitting your general well-being.

Chapter 4

THE FIVE STAGES OF FORGIVENESS PSYCHOLOGICALLY

When most of us do not comprehend the necessity of forgiveness, the form of forgiveness we practice becomes one in which we assume we are doing it for "the other"—usually in exchange for some reward.

Historically, forgiveness has been a misunderstood idea utilized mostly by religion to encourage humanity to let go of their grudges. However, most individuals have an inbuilt need to comprehend and rationalize something to carry it out effectively. In other words, you may ask yourself, consciously or unconsciously, *why* you should forgive.

When most of us don't comprehend the necessity of forgiveness, the form of forgiveness we practice becomes one in which we assume we are doing it for "the other"—usually in exchange for some reward. I've dealt with numerous individuals who adopted this method, believing they'd been able to forgive. Still, upon further examination, it's clear that the majority haven't truly forgiven but have simply ignored and repressed the accompanying feelings. This is more akin to forgetting than it is to forgiving. We forgive and forget; but, what we forget via repression continues to harm us. These individuals have learned to reject any attachment to the person who needs forgiveness to convince them that they have mastered this art—not realizing that this will simply serve to exacerbate an unconscious hatred of or animosity toward the perpetrator or a third party who, in the majority of situations, happens to be the doormat.

Forgiveness is a journey, not a result. To forgive, you must accept that you must do so for yourself and not for someone else. The following are some phases of forgiveness that you may find helpful:

1. Identify Who and What You Need to Forgive

To begin, identify the individual who has harmed you and with whom you still have an anxious bond, either physically or emotionally. Then, determine which exact behavior caused you harm. Be accurate and concise in your response. Make a note of it and dwell on it. Consider the individual as a whole, with both positive and negative actions and their unique life experience. Avoid equating the person to the behavior, but keep in mind that the behavior is an integral element. Adopting a different perspective can help you make sense of a problem. Utterly evil people are extremely rare, if not unheard of. This perspective will help you become more objective and may even inspire sympathy for the individual who caused you harm. This isn't an explanation but a justification. Excuses absolve individuals of responsibility, whereas explanations foster sympathy.

2. Allow the Emotion to Be Felt

Any feelings associated with the destructive conduct must be brought to the surface. To eliminate these toxins, you must find a safe space to express and process your feelings. If the individual who injured you has become more open and you feel comfortable interacting with them, sit down and express your feelings verbally or in writing. If this isn't possible, use an empty chair or another imaginative strategy to release the emotion. Allow yourself to cry if necessary. If you become furious, locate a secure area to vent your frustrations. In some instances, you may require expert assistance at this stage. If this is the case, don't hesitate to invest in yourself.

3. Recognize Why Forgiving Is Beneficial to You

Many of us harbor apprehensive and negative feelings toward those who have wronged us. This is similar to a cord that connects us negatively to the perpetrator and is built on wrath, hatred, resentment, and even illogical guilt or shame. This could result in a love-hate relationship and internal strife. These are all toxic substances that must be released. When this thread between you and the perpetrator is severed, you feel emancipated, light, and as if you are a new person. This psychological metamorphosis allows you to be more receptive to the wonderful aspects of life. Allowing the cord to suffocate you prevents you from progressing, which is why you must sever the thread of resentment via forgiveness.

4. Establish Clear Boundaries with the Perpetrator

You must ensure that you re-establish a sense of security for yourself. Setting clear boundaries with your environment, including the person who hurt you, is necessary to prevent the individual from repeating the harmful action. You need to safeguard yourself and maintain a sense of security, which defined limits can accomplish.

5. Remember That Forgiveness Requires Courage

Most of us prefer to stay in our comfort zones, unwilling to confront our deep emotions because they initially make us feel nervous. Understanding as much will ultimately prove liberating. It's similar to avoiding chemotherapy because it hurts, but chemotherapy effectively cures cancer.

Finally, you must understand that forgiveness is an interior state of mind, not a particular behavior. It cannot be a copy; it must be genuine. Additionally, be patient with the process, as the length of time it takes for people to forgive varies according to individual circumstances and circumstances. Do it when you're ready and don't coerce others into doing it if they're not prepared. Again, exercise some faith and give yourself credit for attempting forgiveness.

Eight Crucial Steps to Forgiveness

Occasionally, the pain is severe, as when a partner or parent violates our confidence, when we are victims of a crime, or when we have been subjected to severe bullying. Anyone who has experienced severe pain understands how difficult it is to focus on anything other than our inner turmoil or anguish when our inner reality is severely disrupted. When we cling to pain, we become emotionally and cognitively handicapped, and our relationships suffer as a result.

Forgiveness is a powerful antidote to this. When life strikes us hard, there is nothing more efficient at healing deep wounds than forgiveness. If I weren't sure of this, I wouldn't have spent the last thirty years of my life studying forgiveness.

Many individuals misunderstand what forgiveness truly entails—and consequently avoid it. Others may desire forgiveness but doubt their ability to manifest it. While forgiveness doesn't always come quickly, it's within reach of many of us if we have the necessary tools and are ready to put in the work.

The following summarizes the fundamental processes required to forgive someone, derived from my new book, *8 Keys to Forgiveness.* Consider how you might adjust these stages to your situation as you read through them.

1. Recognize the Significance of Forgiveness

Forgiveness is about goodness—about showing compassion to those who have wronged us, even if they may not "deserve" it. It's not about making excuses for the offender's behavior or denying that it occurred. Neither is there a simple formula to follow. Forgiveness is a multi-step process that frequently takes a non-linear path.

However, the effort is well worth it. By focusing on forgiveness, we can boost our self-esteem and develop a sense of inner strength and security. It can undo the lies we frequently tell ourselves when someone has profoundly harmed us—like feelings of defeat or unworthiness. Forgiveness can heal us and enable us to continue living a meaningful and purposeful life. Forgiveness is critical, and we'll be the primary beneficiaries of it.

Forgiveness has been found to have significant psychological advantages for the forgiver. It has been demonstrated to alleviate sadness, anxiety, unhealthy rage, and PTSD symptoms.

However, we don't forgive solely to benefit ourselves. Yes, forgiveness can result in psychological recovery; nevertheless, it's not something done to you or for you. It's a gesture made toward another person because you have come to know that it's the ideal response to a given situation over time.

2. Become "Forgivingly Fit"

Practicing forgiveness effectively helps to work on positively altering your inner environment by developing what I refer to as "forgivingly fit" characteristics. Just as you would begin a new physical exercise routine cautiously, it's beneficial to gradually strengthen your forgiving heart muscles by introducing regular "workouts" into your daily life.

You can begin improving your fitness level by committing to not harm—in other words, by making a conscious effort not to speak ill of those who have wronged you. You are not required to speak positively; yet, refraining from speaking badly will feed the more forgiving part of your mind and heart.

Additionally, you might make a point of acknowledging that each individual is unique, special, and irreplaceable. You may arrive at this conclusion due to religious convictions, a humanist philosophy, or even your belief in evolution. It is critical to nurture this perspective of shared humanity to make it more difficult to dismiss someone who has wronged you as undeserving.

During your daily interactions, you can demonstrate love in subtle ways, such as smiling at a rushed store cashier or pausing to listen to a child. Giving extra love helps strengthen the love muscle, making it simpler to express compassion toward everyone. If you practice modest acts of forgiveness and mercy in everyday life—extending care to those who have harmed you—this will also help the process. Perhaps you can avoid honking when someone cuts you off in traffic, or you can hold your tongue when your spouse shouts at you, springing for a hug instead.

Occasionally, pride and power can undermine your efforts to forgive by eliciting feelings of entitlement and exaggerated self-esteem, leading you to view your grudge as a noble cause. Attempt to recognize when you are acting from that place, and choose forgiveness or mercy instead.

3. Address Your Inner Pain

It is critical to determine who has harmed you and how. This may seem self-evident; nonetheless, not all actions that cause you pain are unjust. For instance, you are not required to forgive your child or spouse for their flaws, even if their flaws are inconvenient to you.

To gain clarity, you might examine the individuals in your life—parents, siblings, classmates, spouse, coworkers, children, and even yourself—and assess the extent to which they have harmed you. Perhaps they have abused their influence over you or withheld love from you, or perhaps they have harmed you physically. These wounds have contributed to your inner anguish and must be recognized. This will help you identify someone in your life who requires forgiveness and provide a starting point.

There are numerous types of emotional pain; however, the most prevalent include anxiety, sadness, unhealthy anger, lacking trust, self-loathing or poor self-esteem, an overly pessimistic worldview, and a lack of confidence in one's ability to change. These injuries can be resolved through forgiveness; therefore, it is critical to understand and acknowledge the type of grief you are experiencing. The more grief you have experienced, the more important forgiveness is, at the very least in terms of achieving emotional recovery.

You may be able to perform this accounting yourself, or you may require the assistance of a therapist. Whatever method you use to examine your suffering, be certain you do so in a secure and helpful setting.

4. Through Empathy, Cultivate a Forgiving Disposition

Scientists have examined what occurs in the brain when we consider forgiveness and determined that when people correctly picture forgiving someone (in a hypothetical setting), they have enhanced activity in the cerebral circuits associated with empathy. This indicates that empathy is associated with forgiveness and is a necessary component of the process.

When you analyze the facts of the person who has wounded you, you can frequently understand more clearly the wounds they've been carrying, allowing you to better generate empathy for the individual. To begin, visualize the person as an innocent child needing love and support. Is that something he learned from his parents? According to research, if a newborn doesn't receive adequate attention and love from primary caregivers, they'll develop a weak bond, jeopardizing trust. It may keep them from ever forming bonds with others and send the person on a path of loneliness and conflict that will extend through the remainder of their years.

You might have the option to sort out a comprehensive story surrounding the individual who hurt you—from the earliest stages to adulthood—or essentially envision it as dependent on what you know. You may be able to glimpse the person's bodily frailties and psychological anguish and begin to comprehend your shared humanity. You may identify them as someone who's been injured and has, in turn, wounded you. Regardless of what they may have done to cause you pain, you recognize that they, too, didn't deserve to suffer.

Recognizing that we all have wounds in our hearts might assist in facilitating the process of forgiveness.

5. Discover Significance in Your Anguish

When we undergo significant suffering, we must find purpose in our ordeal. Without meaning, a person may lose their sense of purpose, resulting in hopelessness and the sad conclusion that existence itself has no significance. That isn't to say that we seek out hardship to grow—or seek out the goodness in another's terrible deeds. Rather, we should look for ways in which our pain has shaped us positively.

Even though one is in pain, setting short-term and occasionally long-term goals in life is possible. Some people begin to consider how they might use their suffering to cope due to their increased resilience or bravery. Additionally, they may recognize that their suffering has shifted their view on what is truly important in life, altering their long-term aspirations for themselves.

Finding purpose doesn't imply diminishing your suffering or saying, "I'll just make the best of it." Everything occurs for a purpose. You must constantly confront your woundedness and acknowledge the injustice of the event; otherwise, forgiveness will be superficial.

Nonetheless, there are numerous ways to make sense of our suffering. Some may choose to focus their attention on the beauty of the planet, while others may opt to serve those in need. Certain individuals may discover purpose in stating their truths or fortifying their inner commitment. There is only one answer to this question for me: we should use our suffering to deepen our love for one another and the world. Finding meaning in and of itself aids in the process of forgiving.

6. When Forgiving Is Difficult, Draw on Other Strengths

Forgiveness is often difficult when we are confronted with grave injustices committed by another. I've known individuals who refuse to use the term "forgiveness" because it enrages them. That's acceptable, as each of us has our own timeframe regarding mercy. However, if you have difficulty forgiving and seeking assistance, it may be beneficial to enlist additional resources.

To begin, keep in mind that just because you're having difficulty with forgiveness doesn't mean you're a failure at it. Forgiveness is a gradual process that requires time, patience, and resolve. Avoid being tough on yourself; instead, be gentle and cultivate an inner sense of calm and acceptance. Treat yourself as if you were chatting to a close friend or family member, and you'll be surprised at the results.

Assemble a circle of good, smart individuals who will support you and have the patience to allow you to heal in your own time. Additionally, cultivate humility—not by putting yourself down but by acknowledging that we're all capable of imperfection and suffering.

Attempt to cultivate courage and patience inside yourself to aid you on your trip. Additionally, by practicing tolerating minor slights without lashing out, you give a gift to everyone—not only to the other person but to anyone else whom that person may injure in the future as a result of your anger. You may contribute to putting an end to the cycle of inflicting misery on others.

If you're still having difficulty forgiving, you can practice with someone who is more forgiving—perhaps someone who has harmed you in a minor way rather than significantly. Alternatively, it may be more beneficial to focus on forgiving the person who represents the fundamental source of your pain—perhaps an abusive father or a spouse who betrayed you. If this first hurt has a detrimental effect on other aspects of your life and relationships, it may be necessary to begin there.

7. Forgive Yourself

The majority of us are harsher on ourselves than others. Suppose you're experiencing feelings of unlovability as a result of your acts. In that case, you may need to focus on self-forgiveness and offer yourself what you offer others who have wounded you: a sense of intrinsic value, regardless of your actions.

Self-forgiveness demonstrates respect for yourself as a person, regardless of your flaws. If you've seriously violated your standards, you run the risk of succumbing to self-loathing. When this occurs, you may neglect your health; you may overeat or sleep excessively, begin smoking, or participate in other sorts of "self-punishment." You must acknowledge this and work toward self-compassion. You can do this by softening your heart toward yourself.

After you've been able to forgive yourself, you'll need to seek forgiveness from those you've damaged and attempt to repair the wrongs. It's critical to be prepared for the chance that the other person won't forgive you—that they won't exercise tolerance and humility. However, a genuine apology, free of conditions and expectations, will go a long way toward ensuring your eventual forgiveness.

8. Develop an Empathetic Heart

We develop a more mature perspective of being modest, bold, and loving in the world when we conquer pain. We may be driven to foster an atmosphere of forgiveness in our families and workplaces, assist others who have suffered, or safeguard our communities from a cycle of hatred and violence. All of these choices have the potential to brighten one's mood and bring happiness into one's life.

Certain individuals may assume that it's impossible to love someone who has harmed you. However, I've discovered that many people who forgive eventually find their hearts open. If you can let go of bitterness and replace it with love and then do it with many, many other individuals, you'll gain the ability to love more widely and deeply. This type of transformation can create a loving legacy that will endure long after you're gone.

Four Stages of Forgiveness

Forgiveness isn't a natural state of being. It's supernatural.

Forgiveness isn't a natural state of being. In fact, it's supernatural. It's God's will—His conception.

Permit me to suggest a quite basic method of forgiving. This procedure consists of four straightforward parts.

1. Anger: Recognize, Experience, and Express Your Anguish

Label these emotions as precisely as possible. Consider what precipitated the feelings.

- Who is responsible for this?
- When did it happen?
- Where did it occur?

2. Hate: If You Have Suffered an Injury, You Will Hate

It isn't sinful to hate; indeed, we are commanded to despise what God despises.

- Despise sin itself, not the sinner. Make this distinction to ensure that your hatred is focused on a permissible target.
- Unresolved, chronic animosity frequently results in depression.

3. Hook: Recognize the Illusory Sense of Control

A refusal to forgive creates the idea of strength because it masks your own feelings of hurt and vulnerability.

- Refuse to accept victimhood.
- Forgive the debt.
- Continue living your life.
- Allow God to be the last arbiter of justice.

Revenge is pleasurable for a time but ultimately fails. The agony you offer will never be able to compensate for the pain you have endured. Allow God to manage the matter by removing yourself from it.

4. Heal: Forgiveness Is a Two-Way Street (Event and Process are both involved)

- Forgiveness is an event.
- Relieving one's own pain is a process.

It requires time.

You must continue to open your hurting heart to God, and you will eventually experience healing.

Completing the Stages of Forgiveness

One day, you will awaken and discover that you have a new perspective on the person who has wronged you. Although you may never like or trust this individual, the severity of your pain will lessen. You'll eventually find yourself praying for your adversary. You will quickly discover that you are liberated. Forgiveness is the path to liberation. However, it makes little sense until viewed in light of Christ's forgiveness of you.

And be kind and forgiving toward one another, just as God forgave you in Christ.

— Eph. 4:32 (CSB)

Are you pardoned? Then you may pardon.

Truly forgiven individuals might develop into truly forgiving individuals. God began by absolving us of our sins. He invites us to extend forgiveness to others.

Your willingness to participate in the forgiveness process demonstrates how much you value God's forgiveness.

When It Comes to Forgiveness, There Are Eight Essentials

The Fundamental Ideas That Will Assist You in Forgiving and Achieving Peace of Mind

Required Time

Each individual will forgive at their own pace. We recommend that you proceed through the steps below in the order that works best for you.

How to Proceed

Make a list of persons who have done enough harm to warrant the effort of forgiving. This can be accomplished by asking oneself on a one-to-ten scale, *How much pain do I feel as a result of the way this person treated me?*, with one indicating the least amount of suffering (but still significant enough to warrant the time to forgive) and ten indicating the most amount of pain. Then, rank the individuals on this list from least to most painful. Begin with the individual at the bottom of this hierarchy (least painful).

1. Take into account one infraction committed by the first individual on your list. Consider the following: How has this person's wrongdoing harmed my life? Consider the psychological and bodily harm that may have occurred as a result. Consider how this insult may have altered your perceptions of humanity and trust in others. Recognize that what occurred wasn't acceptable, and permit yourself to experience any negative feelings that may arise.

2. Decide to forgive when you're ready. Settling on the choice to pardon involves tolerating what you will do when you extend benevolence to the individual who has violated you.

When we extend compassion, we make a conscious effort to alleviate resentment (persistent ill will) toward this individual and instead extend kindness, respect, generosity, and even love to them.

3. It's critical to underline that forgiveness doesn't imply accepting the individual's acts, forgetting what occurred, or disregarding justice. Both justice and forgiveness are possible to practice together. Another critical caveat: Forgiveness isn't synonymous with reconciliation. Reconciliation is a tactic for reuniting two or more persons in mutual trust. You are in no way obliged to reconcile with the person whom you are forgiving.

4. Begin by performing cognitive activities. Consider the following questions about the individual who has harmed you: What was life like for this individual as a child? What wounds did they sustain from others that may have increased their likelihood of harming you? What other strains or tensions was this person experiencing when they insulted you? These inquiries aren't intended to justify or explain behavior but rather to better understand the other person's points of pain—the points that make them vulnerable and human. Understanding why people carry out destructive behaviors can also help us develop more effective strategies to prevent future destructive acts.

5. Pay attention to any small movement of your heart that causes you to feel even a smidgeon of sympathy for the person who has offended you. This individual may have been perplexed, wrong, or misdirected. They may have

profound regrets about their acts. Consider whether you begin to feel softer sentiments for this individual as you think about them.

6. Attempt to bear the suffering they gave you consciously so you don't wind up returning it to the offender (or even to unsuspecting third parties such as loved ones, who weren't the ones who injured you in the first place). When we are hurt, we prefer to blame others for our feelings. Please keep this in mind to avoid creating a legacy of wrath and injury.

7. Contemplate a present of some sort that you may give to the individual you're attempting to forgive. Forgiveness is an act of mercy—you are providing mercy to someone who has shown you no mercy. This might show itself as a grin, a returned call, or a positive word about them to other people. Always put your safety first while showing this person warmth and friendliness. If dealing with this individual puts you at risk, find another outlet for your emotions, such as writing in a notebook or practicing compassion meditation.

8. Finally, seek meaning and purpose in your experiences. For instance, when people suffer injustice(s), they frequently discover that they become more sensitive to the anguish of others. In turn, this can give them a sense of purpose for helping those in need. Additionally, it may drive individuals to act to prevent future injustices of a similar nature.

When you've finished with the individual who has caused you the most distress, move on to the next person on your list. Continue this procedure until you have completed it with the person who has caused you the most anguish.

Chapter 5

FORGIVENESS: LETTING GO OF GRUDGES AND BITTERNESS

When someone close to you injures you, you can either cling to your anger, resentment, and ideas of vengeance—or you can accept forgiveness and move ahead.

Who hasn't been harmed by another's actions or words? Perhaps your mom chastised you frequently as a child, a colleague ruined a project, or your lover had an affair. Perhaps you've been through a horrific situation, such as being physically or emotionally assaulted by a family member or friend.

These wounds may leave you with lingering sentiments of rage and resentment—and even a desire for retribution.

However, if you don't practice forgiveness, you may be the one who suffers the most. Accepting forgiveness enables you to embrace other virtues such as peace, hope, thankfulness, and joy. Consider how forgiveness can help you to achieve emotional, physical, and spiritual well-being.

What Does Forgiveness Entail?

To each individual, forgiveness means something different. However, it generally means letting go of resentment and thoughts of vengeance.

While the act that injured or offended you may remain with you forever, forgiveness can assist loosen its hold on you and help you break away from the person who harmed you. Forgiveness can also result in feelings of empathy, compassion, and understanding for the one who has wronged you.

Forgiveness doesn't include forgetting or excusing the hurt done to you or reconciling with the perpetrator. Forgiveness provides a sense of tranquility that enables you to continue living.

What Are the Advantages of Forgiveness?

Allowing grudges and anger to go can pave the path for increased health and mental tranquility. Forgiveness can result in the following benefits:

- Stronger relationships
- Improved mental health
- Less worry, stress, and hate
- Lower blood pressure
- Fewer depressive symptoms
- A stronger immune system
- Improved heart health

Why Is It So Simple to Hold a Grudge?

Being wronged by someone, especially someone you care about and trust, can result in feelings of rage, despair, and perplexity. Grudges filled with hatred, hostility, and the lust for revenge might form if you linger on upsetting events or circumstances. Allowing negative emotions to trump pleasant ones may result in you being swept up by your own bitterness or sense of injustice.

Certain individuals are born more forgiving than others. However, even if you retain a grudge, nearly anyone can learn to be more forgiving.

What Are the Repercussions of Holding a Grudge?

If you are unforgiving, you may:

- Bring a sense of rage and bitterness into every new relationship and each encounter you have.
- Become so caught up in the wrong that you are unable to enjoy the present moment.
- Develop depression or anxiety.
- Consider whether your life lacks meaning or purpose—or whether your spiritual views are in conflict with your current circumstances.

If You're Unforgiving

Forgiveness is something I've struggled with for a long time.

An act of forgiveness promises to bring us on a unique journey of personal growth and change. Among the options you have for moving from pain to forgiveness:

- Take a moment to appreciate forgiveness's beneficial impact on your life.
- Determine what needs to be healed and who needs to be forgiven.
- Consider joining a support group or scheduling an appointment with a counselor.

- Recognize your emotions in response to the harm you have suffered and how they affect your behavior, and seek to resolve them
- You must make a conscious decision to forget about the individual who has hurt you in the past.
- Abandon your victim position and relinquish the influence and power that the offending person and situation have held over your life.

As you let go of grudges, you'll discover that your life is no longer defined by how you've been harmed. Perhaps you will even discover compassion and understanding.

What If I'm Incapable of Forgiving Someone?

Forgiveness can be difficult—even more so when the person who wronged you refuses to accept their error. If you find yourself in a bind, try to see things from the other person's point of view.

- Consider why they might behave in this manner. Perhaps you would have done similarly if confronted with a similar circumstance.
- Consider moments when you have harmed others and those who have forgiven you.
- Keep a journal, pray, practice guided meditation, or speak with someone you regard as wise and caring, such as a spiritual leader, a mental health provider, or an unbiased loved one.
- Don't forget that forgiveness is an ongoing process, and even the tiniest infraction may necessitate revisiting and forgiving several times.

Is Forgiveness a Prerequisite for Reconciliation?

If the traumatic occurrence involved someone you otherwise value your relationship with, forgiving could pave the way for reconciliation. However, this isn't always the case.

If the perpetrator is deceased or unwilling to speak with you, reconciliation may be impossible. In some instances, reconciliation may be inappropriate. Nonetheless, forgiving *is* possible—even in the absence of reconciliation.

What If the Person I'm Forgiving Doesn't Alter Their Behavior?

The purpose of forgiveness isn't to persuade another person to modify their acts, conduct, or words. Consider forgiveness in terms of how it has the potential to transform your life—by providing you peace, happiness, emotional, and spiritual health. Forgiveness has the potential to strip the other person of the power they continue to have in your life.

What If It's I Who Needs Forgiveness?

The first stage is to analyze and admit the wrongs you have committed, including their impact on others. Avoid being too critical of oneself along the way.

If you sincerely regret what you've said or done, try apologizing to individuals who have been injured. Express honest regret or grief and beg forgiveness — without making excuses.

Bear in mind, though, that you can't coerce someone into forgiving you. Others must make their own path to forgiveness. Whatever happens, resolve to act with compassion, empathy, and respect toward others.

Chapter 6

EIGHT TIPS FOR FORGIVING SOMEONE WHO HAS HURT YOU

Forgiveness is the capacity to reclaim your serenity when a particular aspect of your life doesn't turn out as planned. Who doesn't desire as much?

It's unavoidable that others will harm you. And occasionally, the resultant (awful) feeling lingers indefinitely. Forgiveness, according to Fred Luskin, PhD., is a straightforward (albeit not easy) way to improve mood.

Founder of Stanford University's Forgiveness Projects and author of *Forgive for Good*, Luskin, says that to forgive means letting go of negative feelings or a desire for retribution following an act of wrongdoing. "You're letting go of your internal bitterness, hatred, and self-pity associated with a prior incident," he explains.

Luskin has spent decades investigating forgiveness's advantages. In a recent Stanford Pathfinders podcast episode, he emphasized that most reasons to forgive are for your benefit.

"When you recall an injury or a wound that you haven't resolved in your mind or heart, the memory prompts the release of stress chemicals. It results in bodily discomfort. When you recall it frequently, you're chronically straining your body," he explains. "There is a physical cost associated with that."

While forgiveness doesn't always imply reconciliation with the person who has wronged you, Luskin notes that it's especially critical in relationships worth maintaining. "I believe our culture has shifted in the opposite direction, emphasizing the importance of forgiveness in relationships that you do not wish to maintain. "The true need for forgiveness exists in marriages, families, business partnerships, friendships, and sibling ties," he explains. Here are eight strategies that will improve your likelihood of success:

Get Mad, Feel Hurt, and Grieve

Luskin asserts that sadness and fury are natural and appropriate emotions when someone hurts you. Additionally, there is no set period to process and get through the pain. "Forgiveness is allowing unpleasant emotions such as wrath and sadness to enter and then letting them go because you have found peace with your existence."

Examine your anger to see whether it is constructive or detrimental.

Luskin explains that constructive rage resolves a problem in the present by energizing you to respond effectively to a threat. Destructive fury is self-perpetuating and produces no positive outcome. "The person you are furious with isn't changing, and neither are you. Indeed, you're establishing brain circuits that increase the likelihood of anger."

Not to Worry—You're Not Implying That the Offense Was Acceptable

According to Luskin, one of the most pervasive fallacies regarding forgiveness is that the act implies one's support of the offender's behavior. "In truth, forgiveness does not imply condonation. While you may be well aware that what you're doing isn't right, you nonetheless make the conscious decision to purify your heart. You make no justifications for the actions. You simply accept it and make peace with it. That is quite distinct."

Utilize Stress-Relief Practices

If a member of your family says anything hurtful while you're eating supper, Luskin advises taking a few deep breaths. Stress-management tactics quiet your body's fight-or-flight response, allowing you to remain calm and rational.

Moreover, you need to remind yourself why you want this person in your life repeatedly. It's crucial, says Luskin, to keep in mind the good things that person has done for you when they do something hurtful. "People cannot be replaced. It's critical to keep in mind that you only have one parent and one best friend." Luskin emphasizes that this doesn't mean individuals should endure mistreatment or remain in an abusive relationship. That is to say; successful relationships are difficult to establish and maintain when you're harboring grudges, keeping score, or plotting methods to make someone pay for something they did.

"Almost every relationship you've ever been in requires some kind of forgiveness to survive," he explains. "Everyone is faulty—even our perspectives. As a result, getting wounded is unavoidable. We need a technique for letting go and making peace to maintain happy, long-lasting relationships."

Establish Limits

Some gentle boundary-setting may be necessary when someone with whom you share a relationship has caused you pain. However, Luskin asserts that this doesn't necessitate calling someone out, blaming them, or disowning them. "Learn to state plainly, 'What you just did is not acceptable.' "

Recognize That You're Narrating a Malleable Story

In order to protect ourselves from harm, our brains are hardwired to tell us stories that aren't true, according to Luskin. "We simplify to emphasize the danger. We build these mental errors to keep ourselves safe." According to Luskin, the quickest method to forgive is to alter the narrative.

It's important to remember that your friend may not have invited you to her wedding five years ago because the two of you may have been going through tough times at the time, and she may have made a mistake. However, she did the best she could, given what she had to work with.

Assume the Role of the Hero

According to Luskin, linking your current distress to something that occurred in the past is a form of victimization. He cites the following example: "If I say, 'I'm upset right now because my wife left me three years ago,' I'm creating victimhood." A more accurate response, he adds, would be something like, 'The reason I'm unhappy now is that my wife left me; I lacked the resources necessary to deal with it, and in the years afterward, I haven't worked out how to make peace with it.'

"When you convince yourself, 'The only person who can save me is myself,' you develop a heroic efficacy that says, 'I must solve this problem.' I need to figure out how to be OK and joyful in a life that involves the agonizing end of a marriage,' he says. When you can do so, you develop an awareness of your resilience. "When one can forgive, it increases one's ability to manage one's life. Rather than feeling constrained or terrified, you develop an awareness of, 'I know I am capable of overcoming adversity.' That is almost certainly the most significant personal gain."

The Forgiveness Psychology: Seven Lessons on How to Finally Let Go and Forgive Someone

Mary was the victim of some of the most heinous childhood maltreatment I've ever heard about: To hide her father's violence and "keep the family safe," her mother emotionally manipulated her throughout her childhood, regularly beating her and hospitalizing her. She was also raped numerous times by a close family member.

I was taken aback, both by the tragedy of what I'd just learned and by the magnitude of the professional challenge that lay before me. How do I assist someone who has every reason to be angry, sad, and resentful in "letting it go," moving on with her life, and even forgiving?

Mary and I collaborated for more than a year. We gradually revealed the impediments to Mary's genuine desire for forgiveness during that period. Mary gradually gained a measure of forgiveness for her family in the process—and with it, she achieved a level of calm in the life she had never known.

When I work with folks like Mary, it's one of the greatest thrills of my life because I get to learn as much as they do.

The following are seven lessons on genuine forgiveness that I've acquired through my work with Mary and similar individuals.

1. Forgiveness Is Not Synonymous with Forgetfulness

The idea of "forgive and forget" is deeply ingrained in our society, with the implication that we must also forget the wrongs done to us.

This is absurd.

Unless you have a severe neurological disorder, it is quite improbable that you will ever be able to forget a significant wrong done against you.

However, if your standard for forgiveness is memory erasure, you are setting yourself up for continuous dissatisfaction and even guilt, as this is neither physiologically nor psychologically viable.

While we have no influence over which memories linger with us, we have power over our attention. More precisely, we may exercise control over how much attention and rumination we devote to pass wrongs done against us.

Some thinking and processing of the offense are beneficial. However, it is a mistake to believe that just because your mind is pulled to a particular concept or memory, your focus should remain there.

Engaging with and expanding on these spontaneous memories of your offender or the offense increases the likelihood that similar thoughts and memories may surface in the future. On the other hand, if you notice them but then redirect your attention, you reduce the likelihood that these memories will resurface in the future.

Establish and maintain healthy mental limits. Your mood will appreciate it. While you have no control over your memories, you do have control over your attention.

2. Forgiveness and Anger Are Incompatible

It is natural to feel enraged at your perpetrator. There are compelling evolutionary reasons for this, including preserving social order and justice. Feeling angry also provides a temporary boost to one's ego.

However, unmanaged rage frequently results in unhealthy levels of mental elaboration over the wrongs done to you, which reinforces and makes those memories readily available in your memory.

The less time you spend mentally elaborating on your anger and what happened to you, the less frequently your mind will bring it up.

When you become aware of yourself becoming furious, take a quick stop and accept the emotion, affirming your right to be upset. However, ask yourself if continuing to expand on what occurred and extending your anger will benefit you in the long run.

Simply because your anger is justified doesn't make it constructive. Appropriately validate your anger, but refrain from feeding it.

3. Forgiveness Is Not Synonymous with Endorsement

Many individuals who struggle with forgiveness have been advised to "accept" what has occurred. The issue is that concepts such as "acceptance" are imprecise and imply different things.

When many people hear the term "accept," they feel it means acceptance—that you're somehow cool with or rationalizing what happened.

But to accept something doesn't mean you're endorsing it or justifying it in any way. Many victims of injustice are further harmed when they're duped into feeling they were somehow responsible for what occurred to them. That's hardly an act of acceptance.

Acceptance entails admitting that you have no control or authority over the past.

This is an incredibly difficult task for those who have been abused or harmed in some way because believing that the past is controllable gives us a sense of power.

However, it is ultimately a delusion. Allowing yourself to let go of your urge to control the past is critical for regaining control of your future.

Accepting an offense against you isn't equivalent to excusing it.

4. Forgiveness Doesn't Require Reconciliation

Many people who have been wronged believe they must reconcile with the wrongdoer.

This is particularly prevalent, I've discovered, among individuals with a strong religious upbringing. While I can't speak for anyone's exact religious beliefs, I know that reconciliation isn't necessary for forgiveness from a psychological standpoint. Indeed, clinging to it may be counterproductive to gaining genuine forgiveness.

Making forgiveness conditional on reconciliation is a matter of trying to influence other people. Yet, no matter how badly you want the person who mistreated you to recognize their error, provide an authentic apology and compensation, and heal the relationship, you have no influence over it. And it's perilous to spend time and energy attempting to exert control over things that ultimately can't be controlled.

I've observed numerous individuals who are so consumed—borderline obsessed—with reconciling with their offender that they lack the mental and emotional energy necessary to work on the areas of forgiveness over which they have control. To put it another way, requiring reconciliation before forgiving someone has a large opportunity cost.

If you yearn for reconciliation, strive to make it happen but never anticipate it.

5. Forgiveness Is Not a Single Choice

While forgiveness begins with a single choice, it doesn't stop there.

Regardless of how many stories you hear about the "moment of forgiveness," remember that forgiveness is a journey—a process.

- While making a clear choice and establishing a commitment to forgive is a vital first step, keep in mind that it is only a first step. There are likely to be numerous additional steps on the road to forgiveness.

- You will see the relative with whom you had a spat at future family events, for instance.
- From time to time, memories of your trauma will surface.
- Your efforts at reconciliation may be met with hostility.

A single act of forgiveness is insufficient. Be prepared to forgive day after day. And, while forgiving may become easier over time, it is never-ending.

Forgiveness isn't a choice; it's an attitude, a mental habit.

6. Forgiveness Is a State of Mind, Not a Sensation

Many people struggle with forgiveness because they conflate the act of forgiving with the emotional outcome they anticipate. Specifically, most people who struggle with forgiveness long to feel better—peace of mind, less wrath and hatred, serenity and stability, and possibly even compassion or love toward their offender or the person who caused them harm.

However, how we feel as a result of forgiveness is a result of forgiveness, not a cause of forgiveness. Additionally, the feelings that accompany (or don't accompany) forgiveness aren't always the same. They vary considerably based on the individuals and conditions involved.

There is no universal law that guarantees that everyone will feel at peace as a result of forgiving another. Indeed, one of the difficulties inherent to genuine forgiveness is coming to terms with the truth that your emotional response to a significant wrong committed against you is basically beyond your control.

You have direct control over your actions—how you think and behave, including the decision to forgive—but not over your feelings.

While forgiveness does tend to make people feel better, it's a mistake to expect a specific set of emotions.

Forgiveness is a decision, not an emotion.

7. The Path to Forgiveness Is Entirely up to You

After a wrong is committed against us, our emotional landscape becomes dominated by one or two strong (and sometimes culturally ingrained) emotions, most commonly some kind of fury. However, there are nearly always additional emotions involved that should be considered on the path to forgiveness.

Develop the habit of looking beneath and beyond your most outwardly expressed emotions and discovering smaller, subtler ones. These are equally valid emotions as your anger, and they may be more beneficial.

Allowing yourself to feel sorrow, regret, and pity for what occurred, for example, may enable you to view your perpetrator and offense differently. So, as a result, it may help you to think and act differently to better align your actions and beliefs with your long-term aspirations for forgiveness and acceptance.

Accept the emotional singularity of your path to forgiveness.

Everything You Need to Know

We frequently consider forgiveness in hazy ethical or philosophical terms. However, the path to forgiveness is fundamentally psychological, not moral:

- What are the mental practices that truly liberate us from past transgressions and wrongdoing?
- What choices and activities can we take to achieve true peace of mind?

- Which connection to the past is most likely to assist us in moving forward?

To experience genuine forgiveness and move forward with our lives, we must first grasp the sometimes counterintuitive psychology of forgiveness and then commit to our journey toward genuine peace and freedom.

How To Forgive Someone Who Has Hurt You in Fifteen Simple Steps

Forgiveness of others is critical to spiritual development. While the experience of being injured by someone is still unpleasant, it has been reduced to a concept or sensation that you carry around with you. These ideas of resentment, rage, and hatred reflect slow, debilitating energies that will gradually disempower you if you allow them to take up room in your head. If you could free them, you would have greater serenity.

For this reason, I've included a fifteen-step guide that lays out how to forgive someone who has wronged you:

Step 1: Proceed to the Following Act

Your history and all of your pains have been removed from your physical existence. Allowing them to remain in your mind will obscure your present-day existence. Your life is similar to a multi-act play. Some of the characters who arrive have relatively few roles to fill, while others have highly significant ones. Some are antagonists, while others are good guys. However, they are all necessary; otherwise, the drama wouldn't exist. Accept them all and proceed to the next act.

Step 2: Reconnect to the Spirit

Make a new pact with yourself to constantly stay connected to the Spirit, even when it seems impossible. Doing so will allow for the proliferation of whatever degree of perfect harmony your body was built for. Allow God to heal your wounds and allow the Spirit to flow through you.

Your new accord with reality, in which your physical self and personality are fused with your spiritual God-connected self, will cause you to emit higher energy of love and light. Wherever you walk, others will sense the glow of your God-consciousness, and in your presence, disharmony, disorder, and all kind of difficulties will simply fail to flourish. As St. Francis wishes in the first line of his famous prayer, become "an instrument of the peace."

Step 3: Avoid Sleeping Angry

Before lying down each night, my goal is to avoid thinking about anything I don't want to bring back with me upon waking the next day I choose to imprint on my subconscious mind the image of myself as a divine creator who is in harmony with the one consciousness. I restate my imagined image and keep in mind that my slumber will be influenced by my most recent waking concept of myself. I am tranquil, content, and kind—and I attract only those that connect with my best ideas of myself.

This is my bedtime practice, and I always resist the desire to revisit any fear of unpleasantness that my ego may be requesting. I assume the physical sensations associated with assertions that have already been fulfilled. I am aware that I am allowing myself to be brainwashed while sleeping because the next day, I awaken, knowing that I am a free agent.

While sleeping, man imprints his self-concept on the subconscious mind.

—Neville Goddard

Step 4: Turn the Focus from Blaming Others to Getting to Know Yourself

When you're outraged with the behavior of others, shift your focus away from people you hold accountable for your inner unhappiness. Don't blame anyone or anything for your feelings; just let the event unfold as it naturally will in your mind. Additionally, don't blame yourself! Remember that no one has the authority to make you feel uneasy without your permission and that this individual is making you feel uneasy at the moment.

Assure yourself that you'll be able to express your feelings without judging them as "good" or "bad." In this manner, you've shifted your focus to self-mastery. It's critical to set aside blame and even your desire to comprehend the other person in favor of self-awareness.

By accepting responsibility for your response to anything or anyone, you link yourself with life's wonderful dance. By altering your perception of the power others wield over you, you'll open up a whole new world of limitless possibilities for yourself and quickly come to understand how to truly forgive and let go.

Step 5: Avoid Telling Others What to Do

Avoid ideas and actions that simply tell individuals what to do when they are perfectly capable of making their own choices. Remember that no one in your family is your property. Kahlil Gibran's poem serves as a reminder: "Your children are not your children. They are the sons and daughters of Life's yearning for itself. They come through but not from you."

This is universally true. Indeed, ignore any desire to dominate any of your interactions. Rather than expounding, listen. Pay attention to your judgmental ideas and see where self-awareness takes you. When you abandon an ownership mentality in favor of one of allowing, you will begin to observe the Tao's genuine unfolding in yourself and others. From that point on, you will no longer be irritated by others who don't behave according to your ego-driven expectations.

Step 6: Develop the Ability to Let Go and Flow Like Water
Rather than seeking to dominate via your strength, be like water and flow wherever an opening exists. Be more accepting of other viewpoints to soften your rough edges. Interfere less and rely more on listening than on guiding and instructing. When someone shares their perspective with you, consider answering with: "I've never considered that before—thank you. I'll consider it."

When you abstain from intervening and instead flow like water—gently, softly, and unobtrusively—you *become* forgiveness.

Imagine yourself having the same properties as water. Allow your soft, vulnerable, yielding, fluid self to access spaces from which you were previously excluded due to your tendency to be solid and unyielding. Flow gently into the lives of those with whom you are at odds. Visualize yourself accessing their private inner selves, perhaps for the first time understanding what they are going through. Maintain this vision of yourself as gently flowing water, and see the changes in your relationships.

Step 7: Assume Personal Responsibility for Your Contribution
Eliminating blame entails never assigning blame for your own experiences to anyone else. It implies you're willing to say, "I may not understand why I feel this way, why I have this sickness, why I've been victimized, or why I had this accident, but I'm willing to own it without feeling guilty or resentful." I live with it and am accountable for its presence in my life."

If you accept responsibility for having the experience, you then have the opportunity to accept responsibility for erasing it or learning from it. If you're responsible for a migraine headache or a depressing sensation in some minor (possibly unknown) way, you can attempt to eliminate it or decipher its underlying message. On the other side, you'll have to wait till someone or something else in your mind changes before you can improve. And that is highly improbable. As a result, you return home with nothing and are left with nothing, even though tranquility is right on the other side of the coin.

Step 8: Let Go of Resentments
What results in frustration and fury following a disagreement? People typically respond with something like, "I have a right to be furious when my [daughter, mother-in-law, ex-husband, boss, or whomever you're thinking of] speaks to me that way!" and then proceed to explain all the reasons why the other person is wrong and unreasonable.

However, if you wish to live a Tao-filled life, you must invert this way of thinking. Resentments don't arise as a result of the other party's behavior during an encounter; rather, they survive and thrive due to your refusal to finish the altercation with an expression of kindness, love, and genuine forgiveness.

As Lao-Tzu puts it, one must take the risk of retaliating with kindness, or else hatred will never yield to friendliness.

Thus, after all the yelling, screaming, and threatening words have been exchanged, the moment has come for calm. Bear in mind that no storm lasts indefinitely and that within every tempest lie seeds of tranquility. There is a time and place for antagonism, and there is a time and place for peace.

Step 9: Choose Kindness Over Correctness

Given that fact, the Chinese saying goes like this: "If you intend to take revenge on someone, you should dig two separate graves," as resentment will eventually eat away at you.

The world is what it is. People that behave "badly" are doing exactly what they should be doing. You may process it in any manner you like. If you're enraged by all of those "issues," you're adding to the pollution of fury. Rather than that, keep in mind that you're under no obligation to right others' wrongs or to retaliate when you are wronged.

Consider the following scenario: Someone says something to you that you find offensive, and instead of reacting with resentment, you learn to depersonalize the statement and reply with kindness. You are willing to freely send greater, faster energies of love, peace, joy, forgiveness, and kindness in response to whatever circumstances arise. You do this for your benefit, as it's ultimately better to be charitable than "correct."

Step 10: Experiment with Giving

Before you leave an argument or quarrel, practice giving rather than taking. Giving entails letting up one's ego. While ego desires to prevail and demonstrate its supremacy by opposition and contempt, your Tao nature desires peace and harmony. You can reduce the amount of time you spend arguing by half if you follow this procedure:

Wherever you are, whenever powerful emotions arise within you and you become aware of a desire to "do right," silently recite the following lines from Saint Francis' Prayer: Wherever there is hurt, [let me bring] pardon.

As he instructs, be a provider of forgiveness:

- Bring love where there is hatred.
- Light where there is darkness.
- Pardon where it is hurt.

Daily reading of these lines can assist you in overcoming your ego's demands and experiencing the fullness of existence.

Step 11: Put an End to Your Search for Reasons to Be Offended

When you operate at or below average levels of awareness, you devote a significant amount of time and energy to seeking opportunities to be offended. A news story, an impolite visitor, someone cursing, a sneeze, or a black cloud—almost anything will suffice as an excuse to feel upset. Becoming a person who is unaffected by anything or anyone is a lifelong process.

If you have sufficient faith in your views, you'll discover that you cannot be offended by the opinions and behavior of others.

Not being offended is a way of stating, "I have power over how I feel, and regardless of what I observe, I choose to be tranquil." When you're offended, you're engaging in the practice of judgment. You evaluate another person's behavior to be ignorant, insensitive, impolite, arrogant, inconsiderate, or foolish, and then you become irritated and offended by their behavior. Defining someone else isn't what you're doing when you judge them, as you may not realize when you cast judgment on them. You define yourself as a person who must pass judgment on others.

Step 12: Avoid Living in the Past – Focus on the Present

When we have difficulty forgiving, it's frequently because we aren't living in the present moment and instead place a higher premium on the past. We devote a significant portion of our energy and focus on regretting the good old days that have passed us by as the reason we can't be happy and fulfilled in the present. "Everything has changed." "No one has the same regard for others they once did . . ." This is blaming the past for your inability to be happy today.

Other organisms are unlikely to squander the current moment on thoughts of the past or future. A beaver does nothing but beaver, and he does it perfectly. He doesn't waste his days lamenting that his beaver siblings had more care or that his father beaver absconded with a younger beaver while he was a child. He is perpetually present. We may learn a great deal from God's creations about how to enjoy the present moment rather than squandering it in anger over the past or fear for the future. By recognizing the beauty that surrounds you today, you can practice living in the now.

Step 13: Accept Your Difficult Times

There can be no accidents in a universe with an intelligent structure supported by a supernatural creative force. There is no denying that what you've been through has made it to this point, even if admitting it is painful. Each spiritual advancement you make in your life will almost certainly be accompanied by a fall or apparent calamity. All of those terrible moments, accidents, difficult episodes, breakups, periods of poverty, sicknesses, abuses, and broken dreams were necessary. They occurred; therefore, you can presume they had to and cannot be undone.

From that vantage point, embrace them; then, comprehend, accept, honor, and finally transform them.

Step 14: Refrain from Judgment

When you cease to judge and become a mere observer, you will experience inner serenity. With that sense of inner peace, you'll discover that you're happier and free of resentment's bad energy. Additionally, you will notice that others are a lot more drawn to you. A peaceful person attracts peaceful energies.

If I'm a being of love who lives life as my best self, then love must be all I have within me and all I have to give away. If someone I care about decides not to be what my ego desires, I must offer them the components of my ultimate self: God and God is love.

My criticism and condemnation of others' thoughts, feelings, and behavior—regardless of how right and noble my human self convinces me that they are—are a step away from God-realization. And it's God-consciousness that enables me to manifest my desires, as long as they are congruent with my source of being. I can enumerate numerous reasons why I should be critical and condemnatory toward another of God's children and why, damn it, I'm correct. However, if I truly desire to perfect my world—and I do—then I must substitute love for these judgments.

Step 15: Send Love

I spent years studying Patanjali's teachings. He reminded us many thousand years ago that when we are steadfast—that is, when we never lapse in our abstinence from thoughts of harm intended for others—all living beings cease to sense animosity in our presence.

Now, I understand that we are all human: you, myself, and everyone else. While we periodically deviate from our highest self and engage in judgment, criticism, and condemnation, this isn't a *reason* to engage in that type of engagement. I can only tell you that when I finally got it and sent only love to God's children whom I had been criticizing and judging, I immediately experienced inner contentment.

I implore you to send love to people instead of judgments and criticisms when you believe they are impeding your joy and happiness—and to hold them in that space of love. Keep in mind that if you remain firm when you alter your perspective, the things you view alter as well.

A Final Meditation on Love

Consider yourself after a quarrel or significant conflict. Rather than reacting with lingering anger, vengeance, and hurt, envision yourself providing kindness, love, and forgiveness.

Send these "real virtue" ideas to any resentments you are now harboring. Make the following your regular answer to future confrontations: I always end on a high note of love!

Chapter 7

Forgiveness Education to Promote Social-Emotional Learning

Students learn numerous lessons throughout the day, between school, work, and extracurricular activities. However, one lesson they are likely not receiving enough of is how to forgive and why forgiveness is critical to living a happy and healthy lifestyle.

Rather than focusing on resentments, jealousies, and vengeance, we need to teach our children, who are the next generation's leaders, how to be forgiving and open-minded. This section will discuss the research supporting forgiveness as a character virtue, the social-emotional learning (SEL) skills necessary for forgiveness, and some ways to teach and promote forgiveness in the classroom.

Encouragement of empathy in victims toward their offenders is a critical method of attaining forgiveness; thus, fostering empathy can help students enhance their self-awareness and facilitate forgiveness.

Additionally, another study found that a pleasant school experience contributes significantly to kids' happiness and life satisfaction, increasing a student's willingness to forgive. Forgiveness has also been shown to be beneficial in developing various essential SEL characteristics, including relationship skills, which are linked to consideration of others' needs, and pleasant classroom interactions with instructors and classmates. Finally, research has demonstrated that forgiveness is related to increased attachment security and empathy and decreased jealousy. Numerous other research studies suggest that forgiveness is associated with enhanced compassion and emotional well-being.

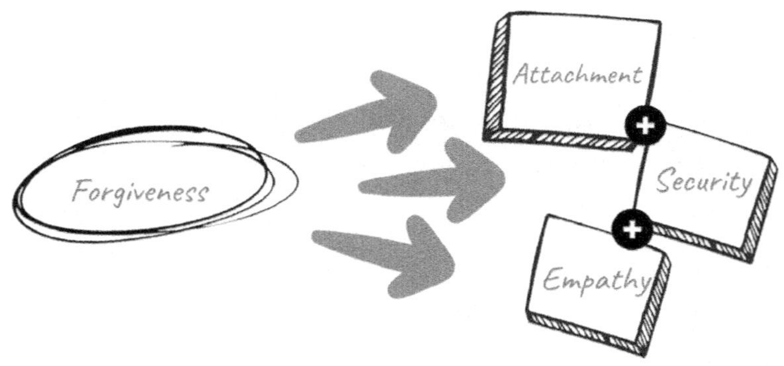

According to studies, forgiveness has been linked to greater connection security and empathy.

It's never too late to instill in students an appreciation for forgiveness. It's possible to find many resources for teaching, discussing, and practicing forgiveness at any grade level. Here are a few illustrations:

K–5th Grade:

For young children who have never heard of forgiveness before, teachers might show them instances of forgiveness in action and underline its importance.

1. As a class, discuss the meaning of forgiveness. How many times have you forgiven someone for a transgression? Do this with a few students and see what they have to say. Then, brainstorm why forgiveness can be helpful.

2. Conceptualize why absolution can be helpful. Then, at that point, outline the advantages of pardoning in basic terms (like expanded sensations of satisfaction and creating more grounded companionships).

3. Consider various circumstances where absolution might be worked out.

4. Implement "I" articulations rather than "you" proclamations.

6th–8th Grade:

Center school understudies might have encountered circumstances where they needed to rehearse pardoning temperance automatically. Besides encouraging absolution in private events, understudies ought to reinforce this quality in a school setting.

1. Host a good discussion by giving understudies the choice to take the side of "yes," "no," or "possibly" on different subjects that might elicit a range of responses, and requesting that they share their thinking (for instance, inquiring "Should all understudies figure out how to code?" or "Should the school hours be shortened?") These discussions permit understudies to develop more mindfulness and comprehend others' points of view.

Host a legitimate debate by allowing students to choose between "yes," "no," or "maybe."

2. Present a scenario and ask students to evaluate the many views and actions that could be taken in response. For instance, the teacher can provide three distinct methods

involving a group of friends engaged in a quarrel. The issue could be one that many middle-school pupils confront, such as difficulty with forgiving. The teacher can give pupils roles and ask them to take on the perspective of the many actors in the fictitious event. This project will encourage students to consider how other people process emotion, whether or not they should forgive, and the latent benefits of forgiving.

3. Have instructors and counselors conduct one-on-one interactions with pupils, giving forgiveness solutions.

9th–12th Grade:

1. Utilize language arts classes to observe how characters do or don't engage in forgiveness in the books they read, evaluate the dynamics, and produce an essay about a forgiveness-related incident. Students should talk in small groups, with each group presenting their critical insights with the rest of the class.

Students should understand that their teachers and school personnel are always there to listen to their stories.

2. Encourage students to form a book club to debate lessons learned from novels with a forgiveness theme (such as *The Kite Runner* by Khaled Hosseini or *The Blind Side of the Heart* by Julia Franck).

3. Establish contact with guidance counselors and inform children that their teachers and school personnel are always there to listen to their tales and encourage them to forgive.

4. Foster pupils' ability to see things from a different perspective in cases where they believe they have been treated unfairly. Assist pupils in appreciating the benefits of not simply accepting and storing up their anger and resentment over a particular situation. Assist them in role-playing a possible path to forgiveness.

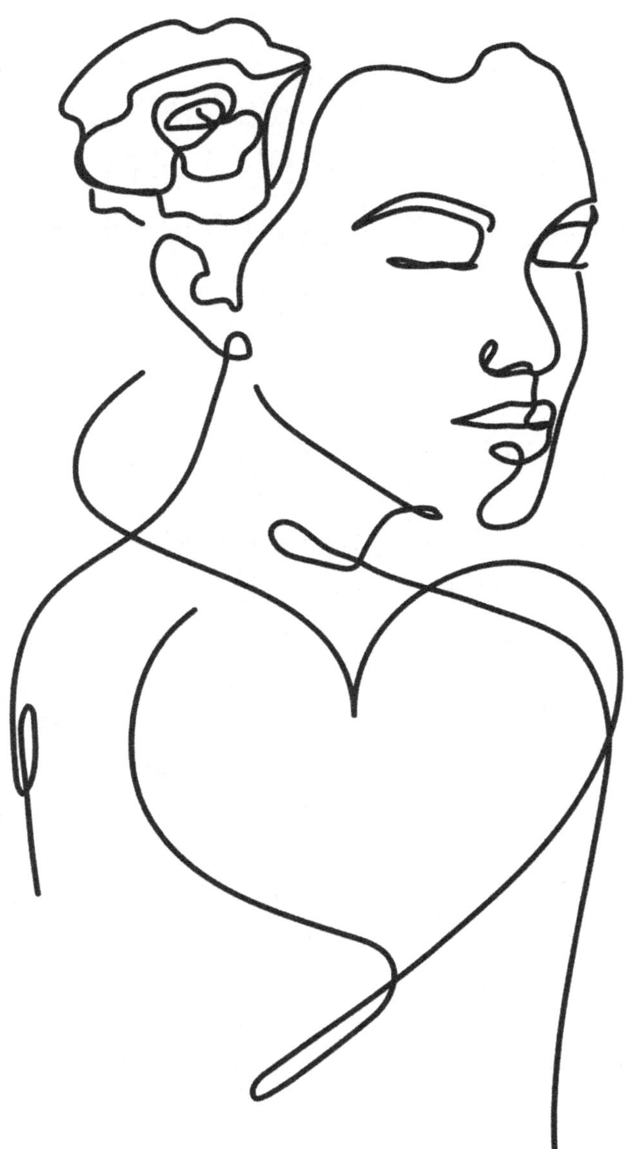

Chapter 8

THE ART OF PRACTICE: FORGIVENESS MADE EASY

Forgiveness is defined as the "peace and understanding that come from absolving yourself of blame for what has wronged you, taking your life experiences less personally, and recognizing the cost of nursing a grudge."

One of the most difficult things we confront in life is remaining serene in the face of frustration, and not getting what we desire is one of the primary obstacles to overcoming disease, desertion, dishonesty, or any other difficulty encountered by humanity. The majority of us never fully embrace the fact that life frequently doesn't provide us with what we desire. We frequently react with wrath or offense when a common but terrible life experience occurs. The majority of us will exacerbate the situation by arguing and whining that the specific difficulty is incorrect rather than concentrating our efforts on how to best cope with it.

We have the option of forgiving the aspects of life that we dislike or continuing to suffer by insisting that life be lived on our terms. Many of us struggle with forgiveness because there are many conflicting perspectives about it. To some, this means that their religion requires them to overcome a personal obstacle. To some, this involves making amends with those who have wronged them. Finally, some believe that forgiveness equates to approving of what occurred.

No one is obligated to forgive; forgiveness is a choice. Forgiveness entails letting go of our anguish about unpleasant situations; it doesn't require re-entering those experiences. Forgiveness implies that even though what occurred was unacceptable, you can move on and make peace with yourself.

Three distinct types of transgressions are forgivable. It is typical for people to believe that grieving and learning to forgive are distinct. However, the issue is essentially the same in each case: something we desired to happen in a particular way didn't occur.

The first type is the most prevalent: it occurs when another person commits an offense against you. This is referred to as interpersonal forgiveness. The second type of forgiveness is termed intra-personal forgiveness. It occurs when you are sad about something you did. In this scenario, you are extending forgiveness to yourself. The third type of forgiveness is existential, in which you forgive God or nature for their wrongdoings against you. Existential forgiveness is frequently a necessary component of interpersonal or intrapersonal forgiveness, as evidenced by the inquiry, "How could this have happened?"

In my opinion, making forgiveness an option may be the most freeing discipline. It's only when we can choose that forgiveness is possible. We have the option of forgiving or not forgiving, and no one can compel us to do so. Forgiveness is a decision to take the offense less personally, place less blame on the offending event for our feelings, and alter our description of the incident to reflect our decision to forgive.

According to this approach, forgiveness develops in four stages.

The Four Stages of Forgiveness

Step One

You are consumed with self-justified rage. You have been wounded at some point in your life and are angry or hurt by someone that you believe mistreated you. You place the blame for your feelings on the person who perpetrated the wrong. You feel that their actions, not your response, are the source of your distress. You've forgotten that you can react in a variety of ways. You may have been hurt so deeply that forgiving the offense feels improper to you. At this stage, there is frequently both active and hidden rage present, as well as significant pain.

Step Two

After being enraged, you come to understand that your hurt and anger don't feel good. It could be interfering with your emotional well-being or physical health. You may seek to mend the relationship's damage and move toward forgiveness. You may acquire perspective on how prevalent the issue is, or you may simply choose to let go of your pain. In either instance, over some time, you will feel no resentment and will have forgiven the situation/person who caused you distress. This forgiveness method can be used to deal with anger directed at oneself, another person, or life in general.

Step Three

The third stage of forgiveness occurs after you have witnessed the benefits of forgiveness in action and have decided to let go of a new grievance rapidly. At this stage, you can choose to experience the pain for a shorter period and then seek to restore the relationship or to let go of seeing the situation as a problem. In any instance, you choose forgiveness because you have more experience with it and see the obvious value in your life. This could occur due to anything as basic as being cut off by another driver on the expressway or as a result of a more complex issue such as an affair in a marriage. At this stage of forgiving, you are aware that you mostly determine the duration of your grievance.

Step Four

The fourth level of forgiving entails the decision to take offense infrequently. This indicates that you're willing to forgive in advance of a particular trigger. This stage frequently occurs concurrently with all or a portion of the following thoughts:

- Because I don't wish to squander another moment of my precious life in the discomfort produced by anger or hurt, I will choose to feel differently.
- I am capable of forgiving myself, others, life, and God.
- I understand how it feels when others refuse to forgive me. Because I don't want to harm anyone else, I'm going to look at the situation from two perspectives: either I can solve it or let it go.

- It's a shame that I'm missing out on all the wonderful things that life has to offer because I'm so focused on my regrets and disappointments from the past. I forgive myself for deviating from the topic at hand.
- Everyone, including myself, acts largely for their own benefit. I must anticipate that occasionally, I will be irritated by another's statement of self-interest (from the perspective of my own self-interest). If I can accept that this is a normal part of life, what is the point of being upset?

Frequently, cancer patients have complaints or wounds that fit under one of the three categories of forgivable sins. In general, the process of forgiving a specific grievance is the same regardless of whether the dispute is with another person, God, or yourself.

Nine Simple Steps to Forgiveness

1. Be able to describe clearly how you feel about what occurred and what you find unacceptable. Then, inform a few trustworthy individuals about the upsetting circumstance and your feelings about it. After completing these preparatory actions, you are prepared to begin working on forgiveness.

2. Commit to yourself that you will do whatever it takes to feel great. You don't have to continue to suffer due to a difficult scenario. Encourage yourself to believe that you are deserving of a healthy life. Forgiveness is intended for you alone. Nobody needs to know about your choice.

3. Recognize your objective. Forgiveness isn't synonymous with reconciliation, though this may occur. Feeling happy is what you're after. Forgiveness is defined as the "peace and

understanding that come from absolving yourself of blame for what has wronged you, taking your life experiences less personally, and recognizing the cost of nursing a grudge." Your forgiving objective is to create peace in your life right now.

4. Maintain the proper perspective on what is occurring. Recognize that your primary source of discomfort may be your negative sentiments, not what occurred in the past.

5. When you're irritated, use a basic stress management method to help your body overcome the fight-or-flight response. When you recall an unsolved issue, your heart races, your blood pressure increases, your hands go chilly, and you lose your composure. Slow and deep breathing will help alleviate these feelings so you can get back to work or school feeling more composed. Then, visualize something wonderful in your life—something you adore. Remain relaxed while the feelings that arise from this vision are held in the area surrounding your heart. This straightforward two-step strategy alleviates distress and enables you to think more clearly about how to resolve the issue that you've been unable to forgive. This is something you should practice whenever you're irritated.

6. Let go of any expectations you may have of other people or your life that they do not choose to fulfill. Recognize the "unenforceable rules" you've created for your health or how you or others must act. For instance, if you have been seeking emotional support from someone who doesn't supply it, consider this: "How many times will I bang my head against the coldness of that person in the hope that they will change?" The forgiving response is to refrain from

demanding whatever has harmed you. Remind yourself that you can actively seek and obtain health, love, friendship, and prosperity. However, you will suffer unnecessarily if you demand that these things manifest immediately and without hard work.

7. Invest your energy in pursuing alternative means of accomplishing your goals rather than investing in an experience that has harmed you. If, for example, you've been waiting for a meaningful relationship with an apathetic parent, look for a mentor who can provide the love, advice, and acceptance you desire. This is what I refer to as locating your good aim. Rather than continually repeating your pain and misery, look for new ways to meet your needs as you exit an unpleasant situation.

8. Keep in mind that a well-lived life is the best form of retribution. A person who lives this way frequently discovers something to enjoy in each moment. Rather than focusing exclusively on your hurt sentiments, which gives the person who has harmed you control, look for the beauty and kindness in your surroundings. Spend time recognizing the positive aspects of your life and recalling pleasant and loving events. A critical tool in this process is making a list of your blessings. The sooner you begin to adjust your thinking in this manner, the less you will feel hurt by life's inequity. You'll begin to notice that the sun still shines, that people continue to fall in love, and that beauty exists everywhere.

9. Modify the grievance story you're telling, and focus on your decision to forgive. You recover the authority you gave the offending event to cause you harm by doing so. When you

can alter the tale you tell yourself and others, you'll be able to de-emphasize the difficulties in your mind, resulting in serenity. That sense of tranquility is the result of the experience of forgiveness.

Four Techniques for Self-Forgiveness, Even When It Feels Impossible

Effective Ways to Recover from Your Most Egregious Errors

Almost everyone has had at least one of those times when they couldn't forgive themselves. You're familiar with them: They reappear in your imagination at random, taunting you. When you said something unpleasant to your best buddy while they were standing just behind you. When you turned in work that was littered with errors to your boss. When you screamed at your child simply because you were having a bad day. Perhaps you cheated on someone, deceived, or stole. If the memories of these deeds continue to taunt you, resurfacing at inconvenient times and reminding you of your shortcomings—regardless of whether the conduct was bad—you haven't yet forgiven yourself. And regardless of what you did, you should.

Forgiveness is critical since failing to do so risks allowing these erroneous behaviors to reshape your sense of self, according to John Delony, PhD, a mental health expert and host of the Dr. John Delony Show. There is a widespread belief that refusing to forgive yourself demonstrates greater regret, but he argues this is not the case. "We may believe that approaching the world via the worst thing we've done grants us additional grace, but this is not the case," Delony explains. "It actually drives us to start partnerships from a position of weakness. Perhaps more significantly, refusing to forgive oneself is choosing to live a life that is less enjoyable, "he asserts.

So, if self-forgiveness is so critical, how do we accomplish it? Delony provides guidance and solutions for finally letting go.

1. Your Error From Your Identity.

If you're constantly punishing yourself for doing something wrong and then punishing yourself for punishing yourself, you'll never feel better. Rather than that, admit that your guilt served a purpose, but it wasn't to torture yourself for eternity. "Your brain has a vested interest in constantly reminding you that you are a person capable of causing harm so that you never do it again," he explains. This is why these errors feel so overwhelming to us—we don't want to repeat them, so our brains harp on them incessantly. However, if you acknowledge that you haven't done it again and that the memory serves a useful purpose, you can begin to de-obsess. "It's difficult because your body has a strong incentive to keep you from forgetting what you did," Delony explains. "You must decide: This is a circumstance, not who I am." Rather than carrying the dread that you'll make the same mistake again as a constant danger, Delony advises, transform it into wisdom: I've learned my lesson and will never do it again.

2. Compose Your Thoughts

Journaling is an effective technique for all types of psychological rehabilitation, but it can be especially beneficial in this case. "When someone is suffering from self-forgiveness, one of the things I recommend is that they write down their sentiments and demand evidence," Delony explains. "Thus, you could write, for instance, 'I am a liar and am untrustworthy.' And then you'd examine that and demand proof." Consider this: Are you truly untrustworthy, or did you commit an untrustworthy behavior once? Investigate the answer in your writing by listing the untrustworthy actions you've taken. You may discover that it's a relatively shortlist, dominated by the memory for which you haven't yet forgiven yourself. "I assume that if that thought continues to trouble you years later, you are a truly trustworthy individual who became entangled in a scenario." Once you recognize that there is no evidence that you are innately terrible, it becomes simpler to provide grace to yourself for your error.

3. Ask for Forgiveness

The chances are that if you committed something heinous enough that you haven't forgiven yourself, someone else was involved. And part of forgiving oneself is communicating to the other party or parties that you recognize your error. "The only way to experience completeness is to be exposed and speak up," Delony explains. "Therefore, if you do anything truly heinous, the first step is to admit it out and accept responsibility for your actions. And the next section is to beg pardon," he asserts. "And you cannot base your views on whether or not you receive forgiveness. You are not permitted to define what forgiving entails." In other words, the other individual or group of people may not forgive you, which is perfectly acceptable. You've made up a story about how you were wrong, and now you've told them about it. What they do next is irrelevant to your ability to forgive yourself."

4. Recognize and Accept the Consequences

Forgiving oneself entails accepting that, while you may have deserved the penalty you received, the punishment does not have to linger indefinitely. "You may have been dismissed as a result of a workplace deception. You must be prepared to disassociate the consequence from your identity," Delony explains. However, in this instance, though being fired is a reasonable consequence for lying, you don't have to self-identify as a liar (nor do you have to assume that forgiving yourself means you were in the right). "Is this to say that you are always a liar? No, this indicates that you lied once." Delony proposes viewing the repercussions as a means to a new beginning: "This was who I was. Future self: What is my personality like now? That is the way to be free of guilt." Once you've outlined a strategy for incorporating what you've learned from your mistake into your future, you'll discover that you're becoming less and less fixated on your previous error.

The Art of Acceptance and Forgiveness

Many people shun the process of forgiving because of the negative connotations they associate with the word. Often, forgiveness is associated with weakness, and it is often assumed that forgiving someone entails approving or justifying their behavior. People have always created a bogeyman out of forgiveness because they were under the mistaken assumption that forgiving someone requires you to push yourself to like the offender or approve of their behavior. In reality, forgiving is a type of mental self-care that we must practice to achieve mental serenity. Simply put, forgiveness is the act of relinquishing blame or anger toward anyone who has wounded, offended, or slighted you in the past. It entails remaining at ease when events don't unfold as planned. However, it is exceedingly difficult to provide a universal definition of forgiveness because everyone has a unique perspective of what it means to forgive. The best we can say is that a person's understanding of what forgiveness truly entails comes from them.

On the other hand, acceptance is quite distinct from the conventional understanding of forgiveness. Before you can acquire forgiveness, you must first accept what occurred and let go of your judgment. Acceptance implies that you are willing to accept the past as an unchangeable event while also resolving to build a better life together. Do not misunderstand—acceptance in the true meaning does not imply that you must forget the occurrence, nor does it imply that you must entirely overcome the anguish imposed on you. Rather than that, it assists us in dealing with any emotional reactions to the situation, including hurt, mistrust, betrayal, and any other emotions you may be experiencing.

Additionally, it's a means of reassuring your offender or partner that you're ready to LET GO of the past and continue your connection. When it comes to accepting the past, you can't do anything about it because it's already happened. It takes a long time to come to terms with an action of which we're not proud. Accepting one another's mistakes is a difficult but vital part of maintaining a healthy relationship.

The Art of Forgiveness and Acceptance – What Are the Reasons for Choosing to Forgive?

One of the questions you should ask is what the benefits of forgiveness or acceptance may be. So, here are four compelling reasons to forgive those who have wronged you:

1. Forgiveness is a Crucial Component of Ultimate Self-Empowerment

Forgiveness is the ultimate act of self-empowerment. The ability to practice true forgiveness is a powerful tool for improving *yourself.* It's not something you do to "acquit" someone but a choice you make to free up your thoughts and experience peace of mind. Consider acceptance and forgiveness a life-changing event that provides you serenity, happiness, and spiritual restoration. By cultivating the art of forgiveness and acceptance, you may truly heal the scars of the past.

"Do not go to bed with a grouch beside you or within you," a buddy once advised me. This is really true. That's quite a few hours to harbor a grudge, isn't it? Before we go to bed, we must erase whatever grudges we may have against our friends and family. We'll have peace of mind, and we'll be able to revive our relationship as a result.

2. Forgiveness Is about You, Not the Offender

While most people believe forgiveness is directed at the culprit or offender, the truth is that forgiveness is directed toward the harmed party. The primary goal of forgiveness is to assist the offender in achieving peace of mind by letting go of the past, allowing them to move forward in life without constantly conserving the anguish of the trauma. Often, refusing to forgive others is akin to driving a car with the brakes engaged because you're resigning yourself to being stagnant, which will inevitably permeate and taint every aspect of your existence.

3. Forgiveness Is Beneficial to One's Health and Well-being

Numerous studies have demonstrated that unforgiving hearts are predisposed to worry, tension, despair, hatred, wrath, sadness, and jealousy, among other things. On the other hand, genuine forgiveness will result in a reduction of the hazards indicated previously. The burden of our past wrongdoings and resentments can drag us down and hinder us from fully living our lives, but we relieve ourselves from that burden when we forgive. The more forgiving a person is, the better their physical, emotional, mental, and spiritual health.

4. Forgiveness Will Strengthen You

It's a common misconception that forgiveness and acceptance are only possible for the weak. In reality, only those who are strong can forgive and accept. This is because courage is required to face the emotional anguish and sufferings directly, embrace the aggressor, and let go of the occurrence. I understand it's not easy, which is why most people want retribution rather than going through the process of forgiving. As a result, only the strong are capable of forgiving.

Consider these four reasons to learn how to forgive individuals who abuse your feelings, and I believe you will approach every situation in life with a fresh, improved mood. It will assist you in recovering from emotional and mental losses while also preserving your health. Above all, love is the universe's only transformative force; thus, love yourself and forgive those who have harmed you. This will make you happier.

Seven Forgiveness Rules

Forgiveness is primarily about letting go of anger, which is beneficial to your health.

We all probably have folks in our lives that we wish we could strangle! Consider it for a few moments. Could you name a few persons you feel have been unfairly persecuted or who have affected you somehow? Or perhaps you have hurt someone and are now feeling guilty or even ashamed about your actions.

Forgiveness is really difficult, whether it be for yourself or others. We could all probably benefit from some assistance in improving our performance. However, we may be unaware that forgiveness is beneficial to both our emotional and physical health. Effective empirical research has demonstrated that when we are more forgiving, we experience less stress, tension, melancholy, anxiety, and, probably most significantly, anger. Anger is detrimental to both our mental and physical health, increasing our susceptibility to stress and our chance of developing illnesses such as heart disease. Indeed, Type A behavior's wrath and fury are significant risk factors for cardiovascular disease. When we struggle to forgive, we harbor anger, resentment, and bitterness, which can affect us in various ways and on a variety of levels.

Knowing that forgiveness is beneficial to one's health makes it easier to practice. When it comes to enhancing one's capacity for forgiveness, there are seven themes that we may all recall:

1. Forgiveness doesn't require you to forget. We are incapable of forgiving and forgetting. Individuals who have been mistreated, neglected, and victimized don't forget their trauma, nor do they need to. They can, however, learn to forgive while maintaining a strong memory.

2. Forgiveness doesn't imply the minimization of victimization. By forgiving, you're not saying, "It's all right . . . it wasn't *that* bad." Certainly not! You can forgive while acknowledging that the victimization and pain were genuine and severe.

3. Forgiveness doesn't imply weakness. Forgiveness isn't an indication of frailty, naivete, or folly.

4. Forgiveness doesn't need an apology and acceptance of your offer of forgiveness on the part of the other party. Regrettably, you cannot expect the person who wronged you to fully comprehend or appreciate how bad what they did was. They may never admit to any wrongdoing. That's acceptable because forgiveness can be used to your advantage, not theirs. You don't require anything from them in exchange for forgiveness.

5. Forgiveness is a process that takes time. Forgiveness isn't a black-or-white, all-or-nothing proposition. It's an ongoing process. You may never be able to forgive another person completely, but you *can* work toward that goal. You may never reach the tenth point on my ten-point forgiveness scale, but you may transform a six into a seven or an eight.

6. Forgiveness is necessary for your physical and emotional well-being. Considering that holding onto outrage is impeding one's well-being and prosperity, and considering that nobody needs to associate with a constantly angry, bitter, resentful person who is determinedly furious, harsh, angry, and unforgiving, absolution is something you should accomplish for yourself. It's in your best interest, not necessarily theirs, to forgive others for their transgressions. You're not seeking forgiveness to do them a favor; you're seeking forgiveness for yourself.

7. The key to forgiving is letting go of one's anger. I have treated numerous individuals who have been violated and traumatized by physical, sexual, emotional, and financial abuse in my therapy practice. I've also treated several people

who had been mistreated by individuals who should have been the nicest to them, including parents, siblings, close friends, and even clergy members. Those who succeed in life and cope the best have discovered a way to forgive themselves and others. They have made a concerted effort to overcome their anger and resentment and move on. They don't forget and don't allow themselves to be victimized in the future. They simply relinquish their rage and opt to forgive (deserved or not).

So, what are your thoughts? Are you capable of forgiving more? Ready to give it a shot?

Chapter 9

HOW TO DEVELOP A NON-JUDGMENTAL ATTITUDE FOR A HEALTHIER MINDSET

Almost everything you encounter is filtered and classified by your mind as positive, bad, or neutral.

When certain experiences are deemed "good" and elicit favorable emotions, we tend to cling to them and yearn for more. Other situations may be perceived as "bad," and as a result, we resist and avoid them. Occasionally, we also judge things as "neutral." These are the items to which we prefer to assign less weight.

In this regard, your mind functions similarly to a judgment machine. The truth is that making judgments is an inherent aspect of being human. However, there is a significant distinction between passing judgment and adopting a judgmental attitude toward oneself and others.

What Is the Distinction Between Being Judgmental and Making Decisions?

When you make a judgment, it usually comes from a place of clarity, when things are simply classified as positive, bad, or neutral. Conversely, being judgmental stems from a reactive and unbalanced mind that wishes to avoid being wounded. Being judgmental is a form of self-defense.

We can be hasty in our judgments, and others may be labeled before we get to know them. Judging people may even occur instinctively, without your awareness.

Can you recall a time when you passed judgment on someone? At the time, it may have been appropriate to pass judgment. However, if you were honest with yourself, it almost certainly didn't feel good physically or emotionally.

When do you stop to consider it? It's not clear who has the right to judge someone. Our judgments are purely subjective and dependent on our personal experiences, neither of which are particularly useful as measuring tools.

Taking note of the fact that you're being judgmental, then practicing nonjudgment can significantly improve your life. Indeed, research indicates that by judging people and circumstances less harshly, you can significantly improve your life's quality and alleviate tension, worry, and even stress-related illnesses.

Consider the specific ways in which practicing non-judgment might benefit your life, as well as how to put this into practice.

Five Ways to Develop a More Positive Mindset through the Non-Judgment Practice

1. Non-Judgment Assists You in Getting off the "Not Enough" Hamster Wheel

We feel a great deal of discontent due to our never-ending pursuit of more—more titles, more money, and more successes. Judgment stimulates this pursuit and fosters the idea that what you already possess is insufficient. When you let go of judgment, you open yourself up to appreciating all of the amazing aspects of where you are right now, allowing you to feel content, grateful, and fulfilled in the present.

2. Non-Judgment Allows You to Have More Enriching Experiences

How often have you dissuaded yourself from trying something new or unusual just because you assumed you wouldn't enjoy it or that it would be an unpleasant experience? Again, this is a normal aspect of human nature. However, when you leave your judgment aside and try something new, something miraculous happens: you open yourself up to the prospect of an exhilarating, life-enriching experience. You might even discover a completely new interest that alters the course of your life.

3. Non-Judgment Assists You in Appreciating Yourself and Others' Beauty

It's possible to see the beauty in everything and feel grateful for the smallest things in life when you don't attach labels like "positive," "negative," or "neutral." You can learn something from every experience, activity, person, and *object* if you're willing to give your full attention.

4. Absence of Judgment Fosters Clarity of Vision

You can only perceive your interpretations when you react to your judgments. By letting go of judgment, you open the door to seeing things as they truly are.

5. Intuitive Peace Is Achieved Through Non-Judgment

If you have "poor" things in your life, remember this: your judgments about those negative things are the only source of stress. When you release judgments, you release the "bad" and replace negative emotions with acceptance, thus relieving you of unnecessary tension and suffering.

How to Begin Practicing Nonjudgment Daily

Here are the techniques we advocate using to cultivate a greater sense of acceptance and respect for cultivating greater serenity, pleasure, and success.

1. Meditation

Meditation is a practice that assists you in developing a sense of detachment from situations and outcomes, allowing you to disengage from judgments energetically. As a result, you'll start to encounter and appreciate things in their normal state (even things that you might have recently thought were unwanted or baffling).

Simply sitting comfortably and silently, focusing your attention on your breath while letting go, relaxing, and doing nothing is a form of meditation. To begin with, this keeps you grounded in the here and now and helps you break free from your mind's indoctrination.

2. Keep a Journal

Self-talk assists you in organizing your thoughts.

Take time throughout the day to chronicle your self-talk. Consider your day's interactions and experiences, as well as your emotions at the moment. Are your feelings motivated by any notions or assumptions?

Perhaps you'll even become aware of your self-judgment. Journaling can assist you in determining how frequently you are judgmental and identifying areas where you can begin to modify this behavior. Additionally, journaling can help you develop a stronger awareness and confidence in yourself, which can help you avoid comparing yourself to others.

3. Develop a Mindfulness Practice

Again, judgment is a habit that narrows the mind, causing you to see people and situations through tunnel vision, depending on your prior ideas or experiences.

Practicing mindfulness, which involves paying attention to what is happening in the now, helps you to live a more enriching life.

This can prevent you from making judgments about present events based on your past.

Whenever you begin to sense a judgment coming on, take a deep breath and become aware of your surroundings. Sensitize yourself to the air, take in the colors around you, and pay attention to the sounds. Take it all in so that you may refocus your attention on the present moment.

As with any new habit or adjustment to your thinking, remaining judgment-free takes work. By following these easy steps and becoming aware of and letting go of your judgments, you may develop a more relaxed, open, and tranquil mind that will open you up to all kinds of new and beautiful experiences.

In the words of Mother Teresa, "If you judge people, you have no time to love them." (The same is true for self-judgment.)

Three Techniques for Practicing Non-Judgment (And Why It Matters)

As humans, we are hardwired to take our life events at face value. Perhaps you're at a party and notice a person alone in a corner, seemingly unconcerned with what's going on around them. You quickly believe that you should avoid them because they are presumably repulsive to others and will only serve to repel someone like you. That is your judgmental brain speaking.

However, regardless of how intuitive judgment is for us, making an effort to overcome it and practice non-judgment can genuinely improve our lives. We develop greater compassion and acceptance for ourselves and others by abstaining from judgment. It alleviates the strains of daily living and even sadness.

Thus, what does non-judgment truly mean, and how can we develop into nonjudgmental individuals? Continue reading to find out!

Human Judgment

From an evolutionary standpoint, our judgmental tendencies have aided us as humans. When we were cavemen, our judgment abilities enabled us to anticipate danger directly ahead of us, which often meant the difference between life and death. If another monster confronted us, we had to determine whether it could kill us, demanding that we act appropriately swiftly.

These threats are no longer the same in the modern era. Our brains, however, haven't yet caught up. This is why we continue to exercise our judgment even when we don't require it.

To return to our previous example, when we scan another party, our caveman instincts kick in, and our brain warns us that approaching someone who appears unpleasant or frightening could result in danger.

What Happens When We Pass Judgment?

To be sure, sound judgment can be extremely advantageous to us, even to the point of literally saving our lives. However, there is always the possibility that what we're judging at face value requires additional observation and mental process.

When we judge, we tend to form rash judgments or opinions. Judging people can imply that we draw judgments about them solely based on their looks, with little insight into who they genuinely are.

Judging can sometimes lead to finger-pointing. Without accurately assessing a situation, we risk blaming the wrong person or accusing someone of the wrong thing.

Emotions and Judgment

While our brain's faculties are most active throughout the judicial process, our emotions may also play a role. Whether we are furious, sad, glad, or content at present, our emotions can significantly influence how we judge another person or scenario.

While external judgment frequently fails, inward judgment never does.

Compassion over Judgment

In the psychological world, judgment is frequently portrayed as the polar opposite of compassion's positive counterpart.

Compassion entails being more receptive to people, situations, and experiences, even when they appear negative or difficult to deal with. When we are compassionate, we don't avoid or despise them. Instead, we extend love and tenderness to them.

Why We Should be Less Judgmental

Being judgmental not only leads to incorrect assumptions and judgments; it can also have a detrimental effect on our mental health. Adults' self-judgment (criticism directed at one's inner thoughts and feelings) was measured in this study, and it was found to be an important predictor of depression and anxiety.

On the other hand, another study that examined the effects of compassion and non-judgment among university students discovered that compassion acts as a mediator of self-esteem and well-being.

This means that compassion enables us to recall our positive characteristics through self-reassurance rather than criticizing ourselves in times of distress. Reassurance then helps our well-being by alleviating our anxiety about ourselves or the outcome of our attempts.

Before passing judgment, consider the following:

Now that we've discovered the benefits of non-judgment, it's critical to pause anytime we see the judging monsters approaching. To begin, consider the following:

- Am I passing judgment based on appearances?
- Am I passing judgment based on my past experiences?
- Am I passing judgment based on the opinion of another?
- Am I being prejudiced?

- Do I have a limited perspective?
- Do I have all of the necessary information?
- Is my emotional state impairing my judgment?

These questions apply not only to others but to yourself. Additionally, if you have answers to these questions, you are more likely to exercise sound judgment.

Additionally, you will significantly increase your self-awareness by asking yourself these questions!

Let's look at some practical ways to practice non-judgment on a daily basis.

How Do We Practice Non-Judgment?

As I previously stated, going against our better judgment may appear odd or even harmful. However, striking a balance in our judgment will almost always produce a net positive effect. Several conscious approaches to do so include the following:

1. Observe without Reacting

When confronted with a situation that puts our ability to be rational or empathetic to the test, we tend to respond immediately, which results in poor decisions that we may regret later. To avoid this, it is preferable to simply go through the motions and watch what is happening inside and around us. Before speaking or making impulsive choices, observe.

2. Consider the Situation from Their Perspective for a Moment

To my mind, misjudgment can be overcome via empathy. Placing myself in the shoes of others enables me to get beneficial insights about them, which prevents me from passing judgment on them adversely.

At one point, one of my bosses at work lashed out at our team over something that was truly explainable and repairable. And while my teammates were on edge and extremely upset with our boss, I reasoned that she might be feeling pressurized by the weight of her job or the demands of her superiors on that specific project, which would explain why she felt our team couldn't afford to make a single mistake.

3. Allow Your Mind to Expand

Nowadays, misjudging is fairly common, especially when one has a strong opinion and is unwilling to accept alternative viewpoints. It's acceptable to take a strong opinion on an issue that matters to you, but it's also beneficial to pause and listen.

By broadening our horizons, we can be more welcoming of others. Picking up a novel or watching an unfamiliar film could be all it takes to shake things up a bit. You can participate in conversations that excite your brain and provide you with new thoughts. Continue to nourish your mind and spirit, as this enables us to be more receptive, gentle, and sensitive.

Judging enables us to make sound decisions, defend ourselves from danger, and survive. However, there are occasions when we forget that not all situations demand harsh judgment. On the contrary, being nonjudgmental can benefit our wellness, increase our peace, and enable us to distribute compassion. Therefore, before passing judgment on yourself or others, choose kindness first!

Self-Healing: Love's Power

Self-love is one of the most powerful and therapeutic gifts you can give yourself. When you truly love yourself, you connect with a wondrous and benign reality within us. This is the truth: we are all deserving of goodness and capable of drawing wonderful and inspirational energy into our lives. Self-love is incredible because it connects you to a sacred and holy source of love. When you're receptive to self-love, you're receptive to the world and your experiences in this existence. What makes self-love so profound is the fact that it enables you to be completely honest with yourself and trust your instincts. You transform into a steadfast source of virtue and illumination for others around you. The benefits include a sense of joy and clear, confident thought for yourself. In essence, when you truly appreciate your body, mind, and soul, you become your higher self.

Many people are unaware of their lack of self-love. This is frequently the result of our conscious (and subconscious) brains operating on autopilot. Exposing negative self-beliefs can assist you in healing and seeing how great, talented, and loving you truly are. Non-self-love is founded on various emotions, including fear, doubt, rage, anxiety, despair, and self-dislike. When we are hesitant about a connection, we feel doubt and anxiety (e.g., *What if this isn't the appropriate person to spend my life with?*). Or perhaps you suffer from sadness because you believe you aren't intellectual or attractive enough? Another instance will be enraged over something that occurred in the past. Perhaps someone *has* harmed you, but as they say, "resentment is like allowing someone to live rent-free in your thoughts."

When you cling to fear, doubt, anger, anxiety, and/or despair, for example, these emotions become trapped in your body, causing energy blockages that might eventually result in illness.

At the point when we center around adoring musings and sentiments like boldness, trust, bliss, solace, and satisfaction, our bodies, and psyches stay spotless, clear, and sound. Self-love is a natural remedy that can keep you in excellent health. This enables you to concentrate on your goals, objectives, and life purpose.

When you love yourself wholeheartedly, you'll be able to love the rest of the world as well. Because you are gentle and kind to yourself, you'll be gentle and kind to others. When you forgive yourself, you express your genuine love for who you are—likewise, for others. Even if someone has wronged you, even if someone has acted unethically toward you, you may forgive them. By forgiving them, you release yourself from anything that stands in the way of your love. Intuition is linked to self-love. It serves as a guide, revealing the truth about a person, location, or object. Self-love is, in essence, your spirit's compass.

To transcend non-self-love, we must catch our ideas before they take over. Meditation, tranquility, Qigong, and connection to a master or a higher source will assist you in recognizing your inherent beauty and integrity. Your superior source will continually raise you. Self-love is an upward-spiraling natural phenomenon! It carries you to incredible heights of confidence and awe. With a clear mind and self-love, your creativity will flourish. Additionally, you'll be able to draw upon transcendent energy and extraordinary life events.

To cultivate self-love, keep in mind that you deserve it. Every single person does. If you don't feel worthy, use Qigong or meditation to address those emotional obstacles. It's critical to purge outdated information to make room for new. Practice connecting with creatures of light, angels, and elementals in nature and on intuitive talks with beautiful, wild animals and the shifting of the seasons. Pay attention to nature. When you are in a state of pure love, it will speak to you and respond synchronistically. Bear in mind that natural life is breathtakingly lovely. Take a break from the hectic and occasionally distracting world around you. Take a vacation, even if it's no more than a mental excursion. Meditating, engaging in soothing hobbies, and devoting time to disciplines such as Qigong are beneficial. This will assist you in achieving mental tranquility and heartfelt affection. This is how one attains self-love.

Take note of your physical body and emotions. Our bodies communicate with us via pain and illness. When they do this, they're attempting to communicate that something is out of balance and requires attention. Visualizing the most beautiful and loving occasions in your life might be extremely beneficial to maintain excellent health. Consider the birth of your kid, the compassion of a pet, the scent of flowering trees in the spring, or the crisp air on the beach as you gaze out at the wonder of our beautiful oceans. Allow that serene spirit to guide you. Then, release yourself from the past. Those stories are no longer relevant, and you now have the current moment to offer healing to whatever caused you anguish. Simply by concentrating on the present moment with self-love practices, you'll find yourself forgiving the story of your past. Reflection—looking back—is a gift. A deeper love for yourself can be developed through this experience.

You are a blessed, adored, and extraordinary person. Maintain constant awareness of this truth. Make a note of it and read it to yourself every day. Write yourself a love letter! Take care of yourself.

Additionally, *smile*! Start My Internal Love Engine is abbreviated as S.M.I.L.E. Consider that each time you smile, you're igniting a small love engine within you. An engine is a device that transforms energy into motion. When you smile, you unconditionally love yourself, which transmits love to everyone around you. Self-love is the secret to living a meaningful and joyful life. Therefore, always remember to SMILE and spread your love to all beings, particularly yourself.

How to Develop Self-Esteem and Confidence

"I love you." According to some estimates, this is one of the most commonly used expressions in human interactions. It's one of the first sentences young children hear and learn to say, and it's frequently the last thing spouses, relatives, and friends say to one another before parting ways or retiring for the night. And, for all the times you've said this to others, have you ever considered how frequently you've said it to yourself? How frequently do you look yourself in the mirror and say, "I adore you?" Of course, self-love doesn't have to entail speaking to yourself aloud, but the concept remains the same. Being a person means understanding that the foundation for loving others and being loved in return is laid by loving oneself first.

In conclusion, when you love yourself, you have the key to living the life you desire. Human beings are designed from an early age to seek love, and they generally continue to do so throughout their lives. When you prioritize loving yourself first, you open yourself up to receiving the love you seek. When you don't love yourself, you don't believe you deserve love. You may even push it away subconsciously. Before you can receive and develop genuine relationships with others, you must first learn to love yourself.

Self-esteem is at the heart of self-love, and it goes hand in hand with self-confidence. It's critical to distinguish between the two and their similar yet separate definitions. Self-confidence is trusting in yourself and your ability to accomplish goals, whereas self-esteem is the idea that you are deserving of other people's respect and love. Developing these two sensations within yourself is the key to learning to appreciate yourself as you deserve.

So how do you begin your journey toward self-love? To be sure, it may come readily to some but not to others.

Because you are the result of your own unique life experiences, it's difficult to predict where you'll end up. One thing is certain: if you want to learn to love yourself and improve your self-esteem and confidence, you're going to have to put in some effort. It may appear intimidating, but have no fear! The accomplishments for which you will be most proud are those you have worked diligently.

1. Take an active role. Finding an activity that you enjoy might be difficult because there are so many options. Endorphins are known to be effective stress relievers and mood enhancers, so for some, this may mean starting to exercise and being more physically active. For others, it may entail developing a hobby and devoting more time to activities they enjoy or are passionate about. Others may discover that cleaning or organizing their workspace or living area is the most relaxing activity. Whichever path you take, it's an action that will begin to teach you to love yourself by demonstrating your capabilities and increasing your self-confidence.

2. Maintain an optimistic attitude. This may be the most difficult to learn, as it often feels as though there is negativity everywhere. However, do you know what? Additionally, you can choose to surround yourself with optimism, which is most definitely available. If you're having difficulty being a self-starter when it comes to being positive, that's perfectly normal. Begin by surrounding yourself with positive people, books, television programs, quotes, affirmations, social media profiles, and podcasts—whatever catches your attention first. Simultaneously, purge your life of negative influences because you don't need them! You're simply inspired by things that will assist you with adoring yourself, and joyfully, there are a lot out there hanging tight for you to find them.

3. Eat well. Assuming that you want to prepare your cerebrum to cherish itself, you will have to support it! Keeping a solid eating routine is one of the most basic advances you can take on your path to self-esteem. Why would that be the case? Since the food you devour significantly affects your general mindset and energy level. Devouring food that's high in fat, salt, and sugar has been exhibited to affect your disposition over the long run, bringing about weight gain, gloom, and awful well-being repercussions. It has been consistently shown that avoiding junk food and increasing the consumption of lean proteins, fruits, and vegetables has a positive influence on both the mind and the body. Additionally, the benefits of a nutritious diet are numerous, including improved health, increased energy, and even some changes in the appearance of your body, hair, and skin.

4. Sort out your financial situation. Cash is a significant wellspring of stress in the present culture. It's hard to adore yourself when you're constantly anxious, which is the reason your funds ought to be the main concern. Even if you don't win the lotto, there are still ways to make your money work harder for you. To get started, focus on establishing a rainy day fund so that you don't have to dip into your savings every time an unforeseen need arises. Then, at that point, investigate your month-to-month spending. Is it true that there are places where you can reduce expenses? Additionally, create a strategy to pay off all of your debt, regardless of how long it takes, and avoid taking out any additional loans or using credit cards if at all possible.

   If you must use your credit cards—and let's face it, the majority of us do—attempt to spend just what you can pay off when your monthly bill arrives. Within a few short steps, you should find yourself in a better financial situation. Bear in mind that a budget is your best friend!

5. Assist others. When you witness someone doing something good, you undoubtedly think, "Wow, what a wonderful person!" And you are almost certainly correct. Fortunately, you can have this kind of positive self-perception, too! All that is required is a helping hand. Consult your local shelter, worship center, or service organization for volunteer opportunities, but keep in mind that helping another person can be as simple as doing a chore for a neighbor or stepping in to aid someone in need.

6. Acquire knowledge. It could be anything from reading an intriguing magazine article about an unfamiliar subject to

picking up a new talent, such as playing an instrument, working with your hands, or learning a new language. As your brain develops, your heart develops as well, and you may learn to love yourself alongside whatever else you're learning.

7. Work on body language. Everybody suffers from disliking their appearance in the mirror at some point. However, making a few little modifications, such as standing up taller with squared shoulders, holding your chin high, and smiling as much as possible, might alter your perception of yourself.

8. Compliment others and accept compliments. Make it a daily goal to compliment someone else. It's not difficult! You can comment on someone's mood or energy level or just tell them, "Hey, you're a pleasure to be around." Their smile will melt your heart. While you're at it, make certain that you don't attempt to deflect or diminish another's compliment. Simply say "Thank you!" and mean it. After all, why shouldn't you see it if they do?

9. Visualize your accomplishments. If you're still working on loving yourself more, close your eyes and imagine yourself at that place. Make it a daily habit, and you'll soon discover that you're subconsciously working toward that vision of yourself.

10. Reverse failure. Failure is a fantastic teacher, even though accepting it is one of the most difficult things to do. It's also an opportunity for you to acknowledge your humanity, confess that you're not perfect, and learn from your errors

to improve next time. Allow yourself grace in the face of failure and recognize it for what it may become: *growth.*

Now that you've established a framework for developing self-love and confidence, let's get started! Utilize these tactics to expedite the progress of your plan.

Self-Love Techniques

1. Recite Affirmative Statements to Yourself

Repeated exposure has been scientifically proven to lead people to trust what they hear. Therefore, why not begin with statements and quotes that will undoubtedly assist you in learning to love yourself? Make a point of reading or reciting these sayings aloud to yourself every day at the same time so that they become ingrained in your daily habit.

2. Disperse Post-It Notes Throughout the House

That's correct; seeing also entails believing. It's difficult to ignore neon-colored reminders when they're everywhere. Make a copy of one of the items on the list above, as well as some of the positive affirmations, and post it about your house, workplace, or vehicle—anywhere you're likely to see them! You'll realize that you're continually thinking of ways to love yourself and even beginning to feel it if you take the time to read each one every time you come upon it.

3. Maintain a List

You can make a list of items actions that need to be completed. Make it a daily goal to check something off your list and then add something new, no matter how minor the task. With time, you'll notice that you're becoming increasingly productive. Isn't it difficult not to appreciate yourself when you're so amazing at getting things done?

4. Respond to Your Thoughts

By commenting on the thoughts that cross your mind, you can act as your own coach. If a bad thought occurs to you, quickly replace it with something positive (you can even have some pre-set answers that you repeat to yourself).

When a *positive* thought occurs to you, affirm to yourself that it's a terrific idea and that you possess the ability to make it a reality.

5. Use the Mirror

Every day, stand in front of the mirror and state aloud five things you admire about yourself. They may fluctuate from day to day or remain constant. The critical aspect is to look oneself in the eye and verbalize them. Extra tip: Smiling while you do it can increase your chances of success!

If you're serious about improving your self-esteem, remember that it's a marathon, not a sprint. What will get you there are determination, commitment, consistency, comprehension, and grace. After the path, you can take a step back, look around, and feel free to love and be confident in yourself.

Self-Love Is the Most Effective Healer

Self-love is the most effective cure. It's the most effective method of healing.

When you look back on specific situations or individuals and realize you're better off without them, you're better off without their judgments, you're better off without their breadcrumbs, and you're better off without their poisonous energy, self-love enables you to move on with ease.

Self-love strengthens you. It compels you to throw open the door wide for those who wish to leave—those who believe you will pursue them as they walk away. Self-love gives you the confidence to know that you can be happy and fulfilled on your own, without the need for validation or completion from anyone else.

You have the ability to be self-aware and face challenges. What you desire is crystal clear in your mind, and you don't hold back when expressing it. You won't accept anything less, and regardless of how much you care about someone, you won't tolerate their games, lies, or false promises. Self-love shields you from those who would have you believe that you're unimportant. Self-love protects you from those who are incapable of truly loving you.

Self-love enables you to be a quick learner. You don't remain in a harmful situation indefinitely. You discontinue activities that are ineffective or detrimental to your well-being. You move away from those who have no concept of your worth and fail to respect you. You don't repeatedly injure yourself by repeating the same mistakes. Self-love enables you to create a wall between you and people who have harmed you. Self-love doesn't make you insensitive; it merely makes you oblivious to people who cause you pain. It forces you to prioritize your mental and emotional health.

The most wonderful aspect of self-love is that it renders individuals in your immediate vicinity helpless; they have no control over you, your emotions, or your ideas. Their absence won't harm you or prevent you from accomplishing great things. Their attacks will never penetrate you or break you because you know who you are and how you enjoy yourself, and others who don't see it will never change your perception of yourself. And when you take away someone's power, they become enraged. They despise the notion of not having control over you. They despise the fact that they are unable to manipulate you.

Self-love doesn't imply that you feel superior to others, nor does it imply that you are stoic or cold-hearted. It simply means that you believe in yourself, that you know what you want, that you understand the level of love and respect you deserve, and that you are unwilling to accept anything less. It just means that you've worked on yourself for a long period and fought many difficult fights to get to where you are today, and you're not willing to allow another human being to come in and destroy all of that. You're unwilling to let another human being define who you are or how you perceive yourself.

Self-love is the culmination of years of healing, years of picking up the broken pieces, years of loneliness, and years of self-doubt, so you're not willing to allow anyone to shatter or even put a crack in that progress. You're not about to let anyone destroy what you've worked so hard to accomplish.

Chapter 10

GIVING AND RECEIVING FORGIVENESS

I recently spent many hours in a park near my hometown with my seven-year-old niece. For a time, my adult self was pushed aside in favor of a younger version of myself, prompted by Shana, who giggles at trivial things and approached the universe with wide-eyed wonderment. Walking through the park, Madalyn and I held hands, sat under a large pine to compare our "tummies" to see which was whiter, made a verbal list of all the beautiful things God had created in the park, took a photo of ourselves in front of a large waterfall, and sang silly songs until we were nearly out of breath.

As I drove her home, it occurred to me that I adored her for no reason. Not because she's amusing or because she resembles me, but simply because she's a member of my family. This intrinsic affection causes me to appreciate her intelligence and her sharp sense of humor; it also causes me to take pleasure in her and desire to do what is best for her—which may include forgiving her if necessary.

This is how God works. The fact that He created us means that He loves us unconditionally, and if you're a member of His family, that means that He loves you as well.

God forgives you solely out of love for you. However, He was not driven to forgive; He chose to forgive out of an innate, profound, and abiding love.

Forgiveness Comes as a Pleasant Surprise

Isn't it difficult to receive forgiveness? Why is this the case? Because so many of us, weighed down by myriad problems, feel that, deep down, we're unworthy of it. We battle pride and humiliation, anger, bitterness, envy, fear, insecurities, selfishness, and other human heart betrayals. Thus, our greatest surprise isn't when someone is harsh, impolite, or unforgiving because this is all too familiar; and, unfortunately, if we live long enough, many of us grow to anticipate not to be forgiven. Rather than that, our greatest surprise is when we're forgiven regardless of who we are or who we are not.

Receiving forgiveness from a friend once took me to my knees in tears, and I wondered how they could still love me despite my shortcomings.

Our hearts are warm when we're forgiven. We're no longer required to conceal our flaws. We can survive despite our flaws because we understand that love covers a multitude of sins (1 Peter 4:8). When we understand forgiveness, we also understand that deficiencies don't signal the end of love; rather, they provide an opportunity for love and forgiveness to shine through the darkness of our faults.

The pardon of God is mighty. It's liberating. It allows the human heart to be simple. And after we have come to understand God's forgiveness, we can share it with others.

Give the Liberating Gift of Forgiveness to Another

Regrettably, few of us experience God's version of forgiveness in our interpersonal interactions. It is something we rarely receive or offer. After all, divorces prompted by selfishness, murders, scandals, resentments, and divisions occur daily worldwide. According to the Bible, people will be lovers of themselves in the end times (2 Timothy 3:2), which means they will not be lovers of others.

A forgiving husband has embraced a woman who had an affair and became pregnant with the other man's child; a father who wronged his daughter and returned home to find forgiveness; or a gambling addict who had an epiphany and was accepted by those in her community, resulting in her healing. Others have experienced heartbreak from receiving more than they deserve.

"There are no words to convey how you feel when someone welcomes you in that way." This is what the woman who had an affair told me. "My natural tendency was to build a wall around myself, as I couldn't imagine my husband would forgive me. I was overcome with embarrassment." She was fully aware that she deserved condemnation but instead received love. Any pebbles her husband could have thrown at her, he threw down in submission to Christ. He exemplified God's love. As a result, the relationship has been repaired to a deeper and more meaningful level. Has it been simple? Certainly not, but it has enriched both of their lives by enlarging their hearts to love and transforming them through the power of forgiveness.

Let me be clear: God may not always call us to retain connections with certain people because doing so would harm our lives and is against His will—but he always calls us to forgive those people (Colossians 3:13). It's our job to ask Him about who we should keep in our lives and who we should cut ties with.

Forgiveness Is a Blessing to You, Too!

At times, forgiveness might feel like a unilateral agreement, as if we are making all the effort while the other person gets away with it. Bear in mind that the inability to forgive stems from a desire to right the wrong, ensure our innocence, and pay the other person. We seek redress! Ironically, we would receive justice if we received what we deserve, but God has chosen to pardon us.

By no means am I a flawless forgiver. Regrettably, there have been moments when I fell short of God's expectations. I've clung to my anguish because I believed I had a right to. However, the forgiveness I refused to extend was causing me pain. We experience peace when we forgive because there is no forgiveness; there is always anger, and anger and serenity cannot coexist peacefully within the same heart.

My friend, you will find peace when you choose to embrace forgiveness and provide it to others. If, instead, you cling to wrongs done to you, the result will be torment, rage, frustration, and anxiety.

What Forgiveness Entails

Forgiveness entails burying a grudge and relinquishing our right to seek vengeance. We relinquish bitterness. We choose not to linger on the wrongdoing of the one who has harmed us. According to one of Webster's Dictionary's definitions, forgiveness means "to make room for error or weakness."

It's hard to imagine a better world if we were all just a little more like that. According to the author and educator Beth Moore, we are never more like God than when we forgive.

Thus, what will be your response? Will you choose to forgive the next person who wrongs you based on God's forgiveness of you? Will you cast aside your grudges and relinquish your "rights" in the same way that God relinquished His when He died on the cross? Will you be the provider of an out-of-this-world gift of forgiveness? Will you allow God to assist you if you believe you are incapable of forgiving?

Allow your gripe to pass, my friend. Give it to God, and then extend forgiveness to someone, even if you believe they don't deserve it. To be sure, it may take time. Commit yourself to God. Solicit His assistance, and He won't let you down.

How To Be Forgiving Of Others

Forgiving others is a lengthy and laborious process. If a parent has abused you, if a lover has cheated on you, or a stranger has assaulted you, forgiving the person who caused you harm may seem impossible. This is particularly true when the individual who has harmed you denies their actions or isn't apologetic. However, forgiveness is something you do for yourself, not for them. Forgiveness entails analyzing what happened and how it affected you, as well as letting go of your anger, suffering, and desire for vengeance. When you come to terms with what occurred, you may move on.

Why Forgive?

Retaining the grief and resentment created by someone who has harmed you is detrimental to your health. Those who refuse to forgive may endure physical and mental health concerns. This can manifest itself in various ways, including cardiovascular difficulties, a weakened immune system, and an increase in anxiety and depressive symptoms. When your emphasis is on the pain rather than the healing, you may find yourself replaying the terrible experience. This negative thought loop can perpetuate the hurt, rage, and other distressing emotions felt after the first offense. To be free of hurt and negativity, you must first forgive the one who has wronged you. When you can forgive those who are close to you, you can begin the process of repairing and re-establishing trust. Forgiveness has been shown to benefit one's health, relationships, and general mental well-being.

Why Is It Difficult to Forgive?

Forgiveness isn't always a simple thing to do. At times, it may appear to be impossible. Forgiveness can be a tough process for a variety of reasons. It can be difficult to let go of the anger, anguish, and desire for vengeance associated with what occurred. This especially holds true if you haven't given it the time it needs to be processed. You may believe that forgiving someone absolves them of responsibility for their actions. Perhaps you assume that forgiveness means accepting the person back into your life and reverting to how things once were. Perhaps you believe forgiveness is unnecessary if the individual has left your life, is unaware they have harmed you, or isn't even remorseful. Giving aside ideas of vengeance and focusing on the past in favor of living in the now might be frightening.

You may be terrified of forgetting or giving the appearance that what occurred was insignificant. Additionally, you may believe that forgiving someone means you are permitting them to hurt you again.

Define Forgiveness

Defining what forgiveness means to you is a critical stage in the process of forgiving. Decide for yourself if you're forgiving someone for their sake or your own. Determine how your religious, familial, and personal views affect your definition and whether you believe you must forget and be free of pain to forgive. Consider whether you want to maintain a relationship with the person who has harmed you and how that would look. These are some points to consider when developing your concept of forgiveness. The psychological definition of forgiveness is consciously choosing to let go of the desire for retribution and relinquishing the hatred you feel for people who have harmed you. Moving on will be much easier if you have a clear definition of what forgiveness is and isn't.

Recognize Your Emotions

If you have been wronged by someone, especially someone you care about, you may experience a range of emotions. You may experience distress, rage, perplexity, betrayal, and various other feelings. It's acceptable to feel whatever emotion you're experiencing. Accepting and allowing your feelings to exist is the simplest approach to work through them. There is no cause to pass judgment on your emotions; they simply are what they are. Pushing your sentiments down and attempting to ignore them can obstruct your ability to work through them and forgive. When you can acknowledge and understand your feelings, it's much simpler to begin the healing process.

Forgive Yourself First

Forgiveness of others must always begin with forgiveness of oneself. If you're having difficulty forgiving someone who has wronged you, perhaps you need to forgive yourself first. It's conceivable you're blaming yourself for failing to notice clear signals. Perhaps you were in the incorrect location at the incorrect time. Additionally, even if you had nothing to do with what occurred, you can still deal with guilt and shame. You may believe that you were harmed due to an underlying flaw in who you are. While forgiving yourself may be difficult, it may be incredibly liberating and beneficial to your mental well-being. Self-forgiveness enables you to provide forgiveness to others as well.

Create Firm Boundaries

Forgiveness isn't synonymous with stating that what occurred wasn't harmful. This isn't to say that you have to forget what occurred. If whatever happened was unacceptable, you want to create a tight barrier around it to prevent it from occurring again. A border exists for your benefit, not for the benefit of the other party. To be effective, a boundary must be established and have concrete repercussions that you are capable of enforcing. By establishing clear boundaries and being aware of the consequences of crossing them, you can forgive the other person and heal your connection. In this manner, you can forgive the individual while maintaining a boundary around the source of your pain.

Practice Compassion

Nobody is without flaws. Mistakes—even unpleasant ones—are unavoidable, but empathy and compassion training can assist you in finding a way to forgive. Concentrating on what occurred and how painful it was can strengthen the negative experience and tough emotions by providing them with undue energy. By focusing on empathy and compassion, you can begin to see the perpetrator as a flawed human being. While this doesn't excuse what occurred, it does assist a shift of focus. Instead of anguish and vengeance, the emphasis is now on understanding and kindness. This seemingly insignificant change can have a huge impact on your point of view and ability to forgive others.

Take Note of It

As an act of self-forgiveness, you allow yourself to let go and move on. As a result, you're not required to inform the person who has caused you to harm that you have forgiven them. If you like, you may inform them of their forgiveness, but it certainly isn't essential. Occasionally, writing down what occurred and what you wish to say about it will assist you in releasing your feelings. You may compose a letter detailing what occurred and how it affected you. When you are prepared, write out what forgiveness means to you and why you chose to forgive. You could offer this to the individual if you believe it is necessary, keep it for yourself, or destroy it as a method of symbolically releasing yourself from the suffering. Writing it down can help you stay focused on forgiveness and why you value it while also acknowledging the experience and the process.

It's a Process

Forgiveness is a progressive process. It takes time to completely comprehend what occurred and the extent to which it affected you. Additionally, time is required to determine forgiveness, why it's necessary, and how to forgive. It's rarely a one-off occurrence. Choosing to forgive someone is only the beginning. You must go through the process of forgiveness before you can let go of the grief and desire for vengeance. It may be simple to forgive one aspect of an offense but quite difficult to forgive another. Perhaps you have no difficulty forgiving one person for their actions but struggle to forgive another for the same actions. Forgiveness is a lengthy, laborious, and energy-intensive process. You're neither required to expedite the process nor are you required to judge it. Allowing the process to develop can make forgiving the person who has wounded you feel more complete, allowing you to let go with greater ease.

It isn't always simple to forgive others. If you're having trouble forgiving someone and it's affecting your life, you can benefit from individual counseling. Forgiveness of others can be liberating. When you experience the freedom that forgiving others brings, you can move forward with a sense of lightness, happiness, and peace.

It's Not for Them. It's for You: Forgive to Assist Yourself in Healing

Healing emotional scars is a journey of self-discovery that can provide innumerable benefits regardless of your life stage. If left unchecked, resentment and self-loathing can be scarring. Forgiveness is the most effective remedy to this toxin, whether it be asking for forgiveness from another person, forgiving someone who has injured you, or forgiving yourself.

Before you embark on this healing road, it's critical to understand that forgiveness isn't synonymous with a clean slate. "Forgive" and "forget" don't work in tandem. To move ahead, you must acknowledge the reality of what occurred.

When you accept what has occurred and understand that you cannot change the past, you gain the incentive to do something worthwhile for yourself: forgive and heal.

Directly communicating your forgiveness to the person who has harmed you isn't always required or practical. Forgiveness is a benefit to you, not to them. To let go of the past and resentment-based thoughts and feelings, you must first forgive the other person. Forgiveness enables you to let go of regrets and resentments that squander your precious energy.

Before forgiving, it's necessary to completely experience and express the emotions associated with the emotional wound—anger, grief, shame, and fear, for example. Occasionally, writing a letter expressing your feelings can assist you in letting go of negative emotions. You don't need to send the letter via mail. It may feel better to burn it.

Forgiveness of oneself can be more difficult than forgiveness of another. It entails accepting what you did and the harm you caused to yourself or others. Accepting responsibility for your faults is the first step toward genuine forgiveness. If you had known what you know now at the time, things would have been different.

As the adage goes, hindsight is 20/20, which is certainly true. In hindsight, situations and the necessary responses are always more apparent. Acceptance and making the most of your current position are your only options. Mindfulness can be beneficial in assisting you in determining why you did what you did. Additionally, gratitude can be beneficial since it enables you to change. Atonement, or making atonement to the person you have harmed or their symbolic equivalent, is a highly effective method of progressing toward self-forgiveness.

If you maintain a realistic perspective on human beings' flaws and defects, forgiving yourself and others may feel more natural. Individuals make errors. We act by our own experiences and worldviews. Each of us is a jumble of emotions and genetics.

If you maintain a realistic perspective on human beings' flaws and defects, however, forgiving yourself and others may feel more natural. Individuals make errors. We act by our own experiences and worldviews. Each of us is a jumble of emotions and genetics.

Consider their life experiences when deciding whether to forgive someone. There's no justification for what they've done here. However, the more information you have about the factors that influenced someone's choices and actions toward you, the more clearly you can see the fundamental imperfection of human nature.

For instance, suppose your father abandoned your family when you were a child, and you recently got a letter from him pleading for forgiveness. Would knowledge of the forces that motivated his actions—his father's abandonment, his youth when he had you, his alcoholism—excuse his actions? No, but it may help you recognize his humanity and forgive him. Compassion and boundaries, on the other hand, are not mutually exclusive. You have the option of saying "I forgive you, but I don't want you in my life."

To forgive yourself and others, attempt to soften your perspective on human nature and acknowledge that humans are imperfect. However, keep in mind that when people know better, they generally perform better. The process of self-discovery that leads to healing entails a great deal of learning to know better.

Allowing yourself to let go of resentments and regrets — in other words, practicing forgiveness — requires that you learn from and make sense of your emotional scars. You can transcend it by giving meaning to your pain and learning what it has to teach you. You can improve yourself as a result of enduring it, but first, you must endure it. To heal and emerge stronger, you must accept, experience, process, and release. When you emerge from the storm, you won't be the same person you were when you entered. That is the purpose of this storm.

Moving on and Healing: Forgiveness's Secret Power

According to researchers that study the process of forgiveness, five factors contribute to our ability to forgive someone who has injured us. They prescribe the following steps:

1. Establish a Definition for Forgiveness

To begin, define what forgiveness is and is not. Forgiveness is a process through which we relinquish our bitterness and wrath toward the one who has wronged us and encourage positive esteem for the perpetrator, such as care, compassion, or sympathy. Please keep in mind that forgiveness doesn't imply reconciliation. At times, it's vital to forgive while also ending a relationship. Tolerating, enduring, or overlooking harmful actions doesn't constitute forgiveness.

2. Recall the Agony

Forgiveness doesn't imply that we brush aside the hurt. To heal from pain, we must first acknowledge the full degree of our wounds.

3. Develop Empathy and an Awareness of Our Transgressions

Consideration and an attempt to comprehend the one who has harmed us advances us down the path of forgiveness. Remembering our less-than-ideal times, such as when we said or did something nasty to someone else, is a simple way to do this. Recognizing my shortcomings enables me to sympathize with those who have offended me.

4. Commit to Forgiveness

Committing to forgiveness entails a deliberate choice to walk in the direction of compassion. This may include deciding to forgive after weighing the benefits and drawbacks of hanging on to the hurt, crafting a contract or statement expressing my intention to forgive, or writing a letter to the perpetrator (which may or may not be sent).

Research reveals that contemplating and discussing a wish to forgive someone who has harmed us is therapeutic. Forgiveness has a ripple effect on other elements of our lives, reducing feelings of grief, anxiety, and work-related stress. When we concentrate on forgiveness, other issues begin to fade away as well.

5. Overcoming an Unforgiving Heart

Finally, resolving unforgiveness requires two unique goals:

1. letting go of anger and resentment toward the perpetrator; and
2. feeling and behaving with compassion for the offender. While goal one may be challenging, goal two may appear impossible at times.

Identify strategies that have worked for you in the past and adapt them to your current circumstances. Make a list of how clinging to the pain harms you rather than the offender. Please make a list of the hurdles you experience in forgiving and then devise solutions to overcome them. Seek out examples of forgiveness and discover how others acquired the ability. And possibly, most importantly, consider the positives that this hurt may have had on your life, rather than the more evident bad consequences.

Chapter 11

HOW TO ELIMINATE GUILT

Guilt is emotional discomfort that occurs when you believe you are accountable for something that has offended or harmed another.

Guilt can be justified—you may have made an error and regret your words or actions, resulting in guilt. However, there are situations when guilt is unjustified—you may have taken on guilt for an action unduly.

Symptoms and Signs of Living with Guilt

Depression, low self-esteem, self-injury, and strained relationships are just a few of the probable outcomes of prolonged guilt. Identifying guilty thoughts and working toward self-forgiveness is critical to preserving excellent mental health.

Guilt-related symptoms may include feelings of unworthiness, being immobilized by the past, having unresolved difficulties, fighting to forgive oneself, acting defensive and distant, and being fearful of attempting a particular action again. It is vital to let go of earlier mistakes to live a full life.

Allowing Yourself to Let Go

The first step is to do a reality check. Guilt has the potential to alter your picture of yourself, your circumstances, and your perspective on others. Before you can be free of guilt, you must first establish the validity of your guilt. Were you genuinely to blame for what occurred? Is it rational for you to feel this way about the situation? These types of questions assist you in determining whether or not it makes sense for you to feel guilty.

How to Forgive Yourself for Wrongdoing

Forgiveness requires self-reflection and a determination to improve after you have offended someone or done them wrong.

- Acknowledge and admit to yourself what you did incorrectly.
- Recognize your remorse and wish you had acted differently.
- Reflect on why you made the error. Were you exhausted, jealous, desperate, or angry?
- Reflect on how you wish you had handled the situation differently, and resolve to respond differently in such situations in the future.
- Attempt to make apologies to those you have wronged. This isn't always possible if they refuse to cooperate; all you can do is your part. Accept responsibility and do what is reasonable to put it right by offering a real and honest apology without defending yourself.
- Come to terms with yourself. Choosing to cling to your guilt indefinitely will only serve to exacerbate an already difficult situation. Consider the error long enough to learn from it, but then move on.

How to Overcome Guilt When You Have Committed No Wrong

If you determine that your guilt is unfounded, make a deliberate, proactive attempt to absolve yourself of it.

- Avoid taking on the guilt of others. It permits them to continue making errors and causes you unnecessary pain.
- You may need to strengthen your conflict resolution abilities to avoid internalizing guilt that isn't yours. Make an effort to be more assertive in disputes, advocate for yourself, and avoid apologizing when you do not have to resolve the conflict.
- Allow yourself to let go of your shame and self-blame. You're not responsible for the guilt, so keep reminding yourself that there's nothing you can do about it but let go.

The Burden of Guilt

Most people experience guilt, as mistakes are a natural part of human development. Nonetheless, the guilt that creeps in and establishes a foothold in your mind can cause significant mental and physical distress.

Perhaps you are most familiar with guilt as the terrible twist in your stomach that occurs when you realize you have harmed another person. Perhaps you, too, battle with frequent self-criticism and self-judgment about your recollections of what happened and your dread of others discovering it.

Guilt Is a Strong Feeling

Guilt forces you to take responsibility for your actions and increases your motivation to change your behavior. Additionally, it may cause you to obsess over what you could have done differently.

If you've never felt comfortable confessing a mistake, your shame may be exaggerated to an almost unbearable degree.

While guilt can occasionally foster beneficial progress, it can also persist and hold you back—even after others have forgotten or forgiven what occurred.

Are you struggling with the weight of guilt? These tips can assist you in lightening your load.

Identify your Guilt

At the time, dismissing your guilt or attempting to push it away may appear to be a beneficial technique. You can figure that it will gradually decrease and vanish if you don't worry about it. Right?

Actually, no. As with other emotions, unresolved guilt can build and intensify over time, making you feel worse.

Refusing to accept your guilt may keep it from spilling over into your daily life, but hiding your feelings is rarely a sustainable solution. To truly handle guilt, you must first acknowledge those sentiments, regardless of how terrible they are.

Consider the following exercise:

- Schedule some alone time for yourself.
- Bring a journal with you so you can jot down your ideas.
- Explain what happened to yourself, or write it down (e.g., "I feel bad because I yelled at my children," I violated a commitment," I cheated on an exam").
- Mentally invite guilt, frustration, regret, and rage, as well as any other feelings that may surface. Writing down your feelings might be beneficial.

- Don't judge your feelings, but rather allow yourself to be in the moment and be present with them. Many circumstances are more complicated than they look at first glance, and unraveling the knot of anxiety might help you gain a deeper understanding of how you're truly feeling.

Daily mindfulness, meditation, and journaling can help if you have difficulty accepting guilt. These activities can help you better understand your emotions, making it easier to accept and move through even the most distressing ones.

Investigate the Source

Before successfully handling guilt, you must first understand where it originates.

While it's natural to feel guilty when you've done something wrong, guilt can also develop in response to situations over which you had little, if any, control.

Accepting responsibility for mistakes is critical, even if you simply admit them to yourself. It's also critical to recognize when you unnecessarily blame yourself for events beyond your control.

Individuals frequently suffer guilt for actions they cannot be held accountable for. For example, you may feel guilty about terminating a relationship with someone who still cares about you or about having a successful career while your best friend is struggling to find work.

Guilt can also arise from the notion that you have fallen short of meeting your own or others' expectations. Of course, this shame doesn't reflect the effort you've expended to conquer the obstacles that stand in your way.

The following are some of the more common sources of guilt:

- Overcoming adversity or calamity
- Incompatibility between your principles and the decisions you've made
- The nature of your mental or physical health
- Feelings or impulses you believe you should abstain from
- Attending to your personal needs when you believe you should be concentrating on others

Recognize Your Error and Make Amends

A heartfelt apology might assist you in resolving issues that arise as a result of misconduct. By apologizing, you show regret and remorse to the person you have harmed and inform them of your plans to prevent repeating the error in the future.

You may not immediately—or ever—receive forgiveness, as apologies don't always restore lost trust.

On the other hand, this process aids in healing since it allows you to communicate your sentiments and hold yourself accountable after making a mistake.

To provide a successful apology, you'll want to do the following:

- appreciate your contribution
- demonstrate remorse
- abstain from making excuses
- beg forgiveness

Continue by demonstrating regret in your conduct.

Even the most genuine apology is meaningless if you never change your behavior in the future.

Making Apologies Entails Committing to Change

Perhaps you feel guilty for not spending enough time with your family or for failing to intervene when they required assistance. Following your apology, you might indicate your intention to improve by asking," How can I assist?" or" How can I be there for you?"

You may not always be able to express your regret directly. If you cannot contact the individual who has caused you harm, consider writing a letter instead. Even if they never see it, it might be beneficial to put your apology on paper.

You may also owe yourself an apology. Rather than wallowing in shame and punishing yourself for an honest error, keep in mind that no one accomplishes everything perfectly every time.

To make apologies, resolve to practice self-kindness rather than self-blame in the future.

Learn from the Past

You cannot repair every situation, and some errors may result in losing a prized connection or close friend. When mixed with sadness over someone or something you've lost, Guilt can frequently feel impenetrable.

Acceptance of the past is necessary before you can move on. Reflecting on the past and meditating on your memories won't change what occurred.

You can't rewrite events by reliving experiences with alternative outcomes, but you can always take into account what you've learned:

- How did the error occur? Investigate the events that precipitated your action and any emotions that pushed you over the line.

- What would you change if you could go back in time?
- How did your behaviors reveal something about you? Do they indicate any specific behaviors that you would want to improve on?

Practice gratitude when confronted with difficulties, mental pain, or health concerns. Bear in mind that people make ties with one another to create a supportive community.

Consider the situation if the tables were turned. You'd almost certainly want to be there for your loved ones if they required assistance or emotional support. You're unlikely to want kids to feel bad about their difficulties, either.

There's nothing wrong with requiring assistance. Life isn't intended to be confronted alone.

Rather than feeling guilty during times of difficulty, cultivate thankfulness by:

- Expressing gratitude to loved ones for their compassion.
- Expressing your gratitude plainly.
- Expressing gratitude for any possibilities earned as a result of others' assistance.
- Committing to repaying this assistance once you've regained your footing.

Substitute Self-Compassion for Critical Self-Talk

Making a mistake doesn't automatically make you a horrible person; everyone makes mistakes from time to time.

Guilt can elicit some pretty harsh self-criticism, but lecturing yourself on how you screwed up won't make things better. While you may encounter some external penalties, self-punishment frequently imposes the greatest emotional toll.

Rather than condemning yourself, consider what you would say to a friend in a similar position. Perhaps you'd highlight their accomplishments, remind them of their strengths, and express your appreciation for them.

You Are Deserving of the Same Consideration

A person's life and the circumstances in which they find themself are both complicated. You may be responsible for your error, but so may the others.

Reminding yourself of your worth can enhance your confidence, allowing you to think more clearly and avoid being misled by emotional misery.

Remorse Can Work in Your Favor

Guilt can act as a warning system, alerting you when you've made a choice that contradicts your values. Rather than allowing it to overwhelm you, consider putting it to work.

When handled effectively, guilt can shed light on areas of yourself with which you are dissatisfied.

Perhaps you struggled with honesty and were caught in a lie. Perhaps you'd like to spend more time with your family, but something always comes up.

Taking action to solve those situations can help you move closer to your goals.

If you're feeling bad about not spending enough time with pals, you may make more effort to connect. When stress causes you to lose focus on your relationship, you may benefit from committing one night a week to your partner.

What guilt has to say about you is also important to take note of.

Regret about injuring another person demonstrates that you possess empathy and don't mean harm. Thus, affecting change in your life may entail concentrating on strategies to avoid repeating that error.

If you frequently feel guilty about things you have no control over, it may be good to work with a professional to determine the source of your guilt.

Forgive Yourself

Self-forgiveness is critical for developing self-compassion. When you forgive yourself, you, like all other humans, accept that you made a mistake. Then, you may look forward without allowing that error to define you. By accepting your imperfect self, you show yourself love and kindness.

Self-forgiveness entails four critical steps:

1. Accept accountability for your actions.
2. Express regret and remorse without allowing these feelings to turn into humiliation.
3. Commit to atoning for any hurt you have caused.
4. Develop self-acceptance and confidence in your ability to improve in the future.

Consult with People You Trust

Individuals frequently have difficulty discussing guilt, which is normal. After all, it's not easy to talk about a regrettable error. This means that guilt can cause you to withdraw, and loneliness and isolation are likely to obstruct the healing process.

While it's understandable to be concerned about how people will react to what happened, you may be surprised by their responses. Indeed, you may discover that family and friends provide significant assistance.

Generally, those that care about you will show you kindness and compassion. Additionally, communicating unpleasant or painful emotions frequently alleviates tension.

Additionally, friends and relatives might assist you in feeling less alone by sharing their own experiences. Almost everyone has done something they regret, and as a result, most people understand what it's like to feel guilty.

The outside viewpoint can also be quite beneficial, particularly if you are experiencing survivor guilt or guilt over something you had no control over.

Consult a Therapist

Severe or persistent guilt isn't always easy to overcome. Certain individuals have difficulty working through feelings of guilt associated with:

- Intrusive thoughts
- Depression
- Psychological distress or abuser's difficult to open up about guilt if you're afraid of being judged.

Avoiding these sentiments, on the other hand, frequently exacerbates the condition. Guilt may have a detrimental effect on relationships and add stress to daily life. Additionally, it may contribute to sleep difficulties and mental health concerns. Alternatively, it can result in coping mechanisms like substance abuse.

When an undercurrent of sorrow, rumination, and regret pervades your daily interactions, preventing you from remaining present with yourself and others, seeking professional assistance may be a wise next step.

A therapist can provide support by assisting you in identifying and addressing the sources of your guilt, developing appropriate coping techniques, and increasing your self-compassion.

You can begin letting go by improving your resilience and developing the confidence necessary to make better future decisions. Guilt can be a thing of the past!

If you're fighting to overcome guilt, realize that you're not alone. Therapy can provide a secure environment to practice forgiving yourself and move forward.

Forgive Yourself: Let Go of Shame And Regrets from the Past

Allow yourself forgiveness. Allow it to pass. Ignore it. Proceed. It's simple to say, but so much more difficult to do! We all make mistakes occasionally, whether it's lashing out at a buddy, self-destructive conduct, or cutting costs at work. And frequently, these errors are accompanied by intense emotions of shame, self-condemnation, and humiliation.

Counselors and life coaches have discovered that if these emotions aren't addressed, they can result in stress, sadness, anxiety disorders, and even heart disease. Not exactly the recipe for happiness! Fortunately, by learning to forgive yourself and letting go of the guilt, you can avoid these harmful consequences and live a better life.

How Is Forgiveness Defined? Why Is It So Critical?

Forgiveness is a conscious choice to release unpleasant emotions toward oneself or another person. Before extending forgiveness, you may experience the following unpleasant emotions: guilt, shame, self-condemnation, humiliation, and bitterness.

Forgiveness of errors or wrongdoings is critical to your well-being. According to Dr. Frederic Luskin of Stanford University, "Learning to forgive helps people experience less pain, less anger, less stress, and less sadness" Individuals who develop the capacity to forgive report much fewer stress-related symptoms such as backache, muscle tension, dizziness, migraines, and upset stomach. Additionally, individuals report an increase in appetite, sleep patterns, vitality, and overall well-being."

Allowing yourself and others to forgive lets you let go of negativity and concentrate on a more optimistic future. Additionally, it assists you in strengthening bonds with the people closest to you.

Why Is Self-Forgiveness So Difficult to Accomplish?

Too frequently, we punish ourselves for previous errors, as if we might somehow make up for our transgressions. Throughout the course of the day, we feel like we're falling short. We refer to ourselves as losers, seeing ourselves as unfit. We are tethered to our pasts, clinging to our traumas and grudges. And, while no one else is aware of our private anguish, the negative feelings we experience sap our joy and contentment in life.

According to counselors and life coaches, the most difficult person to forgive is yourself. Not the one who betrayed you. Or the absent father. Or even the ex-lover who tore your heart to shreds.

Why? Because you are aware of yourself and interact with yourself daily. Consider this.

How to Accept Forgiveness: Four Tips for Those Stuck in Past Mistakes

1. Talk About It

Silence can be lethal when it comes to the past. Therefore, quit faking. Break free from the shackles of self-containment and speak about what's ripping you apart on the inside. Communicate your emotions to a counselor, mentor, or trusted friend. Forgiveness begins with being open and transparent about your true self, sharing both the good and the bad. Therefore, say what has to be said.

2. Be Truthful to Yourself

We frequently believe that if we simply pretend it never occurred, it will all go away. That does seem pleasant . . . but sadly, this isn't the least bit true. Choose to emerge from denial and take a proactive stance. Be forthright about how you erred and the repercussions of your actions. Create a journal entry detailing the exact behaviors and activities causing you distress.

3. Accept It for What It Is

You will make blunders in life as an imperfect human. Accept it. At times, you'll injure others. You'll regret it. It's a natural consequence of living in a less-than-ideal world. However, you *do* have an option.

Either you embrace your past and feel the freedom to move on and enjoy the present, or you accept it as it is and experience the freedom to move on and enjoy the now. Acceptance of oneself is vital for emotional well-being, so don't miss out!

4. Let Go

Refrain from harboring guilt. You're not required to justify your previous acts or make a case for yourself. Allowing yourself to let go of the past entails burying it and relinquishing your right to self-condemnation. Bestowing forgiveness is a choice, but it's also a journey. It's a matter of deciding to stop hating or shaming yourself and instead begin to see yourself as a valuable human being.

Creating Reasonable Expectations

Evaluate the standards you (and others) have set for yourself. Are they in good health? Or are they implausible?

If you discover that you can never measure up—regardless of how hard you try—you may simply need to alter your approach to life. Healthy expectations are attainable and rewarding, rather than depleting and overpowering.

Make a Compromise with Yourself

It's time to reach an agreement with yourself to . . .

- Permit yourself to relinquish the past and focus on the present.
- Stop beating yourself up over something that happened two, five, or ten years ago.
- Eliminate guilt and shame from your thoughts and behaviors.
- Accept and respect yourself as you are . . . despite your mistakes.

To forgive is to liberate a captive and learn that the captive was you!

Chapter 12

HEALING YOUR INNER CHILD

Have you ever listened to the small voice within you? No matter our age, we carry our younger selves with us daily. Perhaps our devastated five-year-old self emerges when our dearest friend fails to return our phone call, or our bewildered fifteen-year-old self emerges when a coworker disagrees with us. Inner child work is all about caring for this younger version of ourselves.

What Is the Purpose of Inner Child Work?

Inner child work, also known as *inner child healing,* is a technique for addressing unmet needs as children and mending attachment scars. We all have a younger self that was never loved in the way they needed to be loved. Inner child work, like any other sort of inner work, entails establishing an environment in which your subconscious can take the lead. Inner work explores our genuine sentiments and aspects of ourselves that have been rejected and categorized as "inappropriate" or "too much" by others. Allowing ourselves time to venture within enables us to address our inappropriate coping techniques (avoidance, suppressing our feelings, etc.) and completely accept and integrate our subconscious.

Inner Child Work Is a Form of Treatment

Numerous methods of treatment incorporate inner child work. The inner child lens can be found in various settings, including trauma therapy, Parts Work, Internal Family Systems, EMDR, sensorimotor psychotherapy, somatic work, Gestalt work, art therapy, and story or narrative therapy.

What makes inner child work genuinely unique is its purpose of communicating with our inner child in their language. This language is emotionally grounded and embodied rather than intellectually conveyed through thoughts and words.

What Exactly Does "Inner Child" Mean?

Our inner child depicts ourselves at various stages of our childhood, and they can be of any age. This aspect is inextricably linked to our innate excitement, curiosity, and creativity as youngsters. By connecting with your inner child, you may access their characteristics and experiences at the moment. You can even feel how they felt physically.

We are also quite impressionable as children, rapidly absorbing what our settings and caregivers teach us and how they treat us. Inner child wounds, also known as attachment wounds, can emerge from a traumatic experience or a chronic rupture that cannot be repaired. For children, an unrepaired rupture can appear as a cry for aid that goes unnoticed by an emotionally inaccessible caregiver. As adults, ruptures also occur in our daily lives, from when someone forgets to hold the door for us at the store to when a friend fails to greet us.

We internalize them and decide whether the event remains a wound or is processed immediately.

Adulthood provides us with the opportunity to heal our injured inner child and build the safe, secure inner and outward environments that our younger self desires.

Why Is It Necessary to Cure the Inner Child?

As adults, we carry childhood traumas, whether basic or complex, ranging from emotional neglect to physical violence. Many adults believe they are alone in their wounds and feelings, hence concealing them in the belief that this is a natural aspect of adulthood.

By mending our inner child, we can begin to generate the sense of comfort and safety that our younger selves have always craved. By doing so, we give our inner child's positive characteristics a chance to shine. We discover our inherent abilities, inner curiosity, and infinite potential for love.

Signs That Your Inner Child Needs Healing

The following symptoms are associated with the original attachment wounds:

1. Excessive Reactivity

When our wounded inner child manifests in our daily life, we can recognize it when we find ourselves excessively reacting to situations, suddenly feeling distant or angered.

2. Overvaluing Independence

This can manifest as reiterating the narrative "I don't need anyone" and refusing to accept assistance.

3. Self-Destructive Coping Strategies

This can manifest as excessive drinking, shopping, infidelity, gambling, overeating, or chronic procrastination.

4. Inadequate Emotional and Mental Well-Being

This can express itself in a multitude of ways, the most common of which are as follows:

- Depression
- Lacking motivation
- Self-isolation
- Insomnia
- Weight gain or loss
- Inability to concentrate or be productive at work
- Sleep problems

Individuals who have had attachment wounds as children frequently unintentionally reproduce attachment patterns in their adult relationships, whether romantic or not. This essentially indicates that they are repeating patterns of childhood trauma.

It's suggested that we learn to listen and speak in the bodily language of our inner child as a means to better understand them.

Consider what it's like to play with a child. You'll recall that rather than speaking to you incomplete, eloquent sentences, children communicate their desires and needs through body language and intuitive noises. That is why a large part of reconnecting with our inner child involves engaging in activities that engage all of our senses. When we can be present in a situation rather than reasoning our way through it, we're bound to succeed.

We can begin by transitioning from our left brain—which is linked with language, logic, and critical thinking—to our right brain, related to emotional expression, intuition, and creativity. The following are some suggestions for getting started:

1. Engage in Breathwork and Mindfulness Exercises

Connecting with our deep breaths and physical body enables us to disengage from the stresses of adulthood and sympathetic" "fight-or-flight" arousal, allowing us to be curious about the present.

Utilize all five senses to maintain contact with our bodies. This can be accomplished by taking three deliberate deep breaths. Placing one hand on your stomach and chest can be beneficial.

Take note of one thing you notice as you settle in.
There is one thing you smell.
You hear one thing.
You taste only one thing.
You are aware of one thing.

2. Encourage your Inventiveness

Allowing ourselves to sketch, cook, garden, sit, or read graphic novels centers and reconnects us with our inner child.

3. Collect Something

Do you recall how it felt to collect items as a child? Collecting items found on our walk to the beach (sticks, rocks, shells) can help us reconnect with our inner child. This isn't for practical reasons; rather, we do so for the sake of pure experience. Are you unsure of what to collect? As adults, many of us amass book collections. The good news is that you don't have to read them to enjoy them!

4. Develop your Visualization Skills

Visualization is an excellent technique to reconnect with your inner child. Visualizations assist us in accessing our imagination and sensory faculties. When first beginning, guided visualizations can be extremely beneficial.

5. Journal

Journaling's purpose is to establish a secure environment for you (and, in this case, your inner child) to express yourself honestly without regard for the outside world's expectations. It can take the form of just sitting down and inquiring how your inner child is feeling today. The trick allows your inner child to perceive their own experiences without censoring or correcting them.

Exploring Your Inner Child

No one is returning for the inner kid. With the exception of you.

—Tanya Markul

Everyone possesses an inner child. You *are* your inner kid, but it's not the infantile mentality you have clung to for years. This is your subconscious mind at work. You possess all of the suppressed memories and emotions from your childhood that occasionally return. Healing your inner child is critical for overall health and development.

According to the American Psychological Association, "research has established that connections between parents, caregivers, and children and adolescents that:

- Are affable, receptive, and communicative;
- Include reasonable constraints, and
- Justify behavioral rules

are related with increased self-esteem, improved academic achievement, and fewer negative consequences such as depression or substance abuse in children and adolescents."

Relationships with caregivers affect one's social, cognitive, emotional, and mental health. What happens when a caregiver doesn't provide a child with a supportive relationship? Your inner child is mainly motivated by an unsatisfied childhood longing for unconditional love and safety. You are most influenced during your early years of life by the caretakers who surround you. If your inner child is provoked, triggers, trauma responses, and self-protective strategies may come into play.

If Jane seeks validation from her husband and he is too busy to compliment her, she may feel unnoticed and unheard. Perhaps her inner child's yearning for attention is stirred. Jane then begins a battle over something that appears insignificant to others but is significant to her. Even if her husband had no intention of hurting her, she feels rejected. This type of reaction frequently occurs when the inner child is triggered. Anger emerges as a secondary emotion.

Even if you are now in a stronger relationship, you experience the sensations of abandonment. Due to the projection of past pain, intimacy may be more difficult to master. These triggers might also be as simple as feeling overwhelmed, stressed, or unappreciated. Each person has a unique set of triggers.

Additionally, trauma responses may manifest in the following ways:

- Refusal to seek assistance
- Saying "I'm fine" when you're not
- Feeling like a burden

Your self-protective behaviors may include perfectionism, people-pleasing, and power-hunger, among others. This might emerge in a variety of ways as you attempt to compensate for the neglect you endured as a child. You feel insufficient as you are, and so you strive even harder, and repression exacerbates the problem. Your inner kid will eventually find a way out. It can manifest as anxiety, depression, post-traumatic stress disorder (PTSD), emotional dysregulation, impulsivity, outbursts, trouble functioning, and social disengagement. Ignoring it only strengthens it. It is frequently attempting to inform you that something is wrong. If it begins to take over your life, it is important to get treatment from a mental health expert.

Unresolved Trauma

Unresolved trauma may be at the heart of your difficulties. Trauma can take on a variety of forms. Aundi Kolber defines "Big Trauma" as "events such as abuse, neglect, natural disaster, serious accident, or feeling of loss." Then there's "insignificant trauma." "That's when things happen that may appear as minor as a paper cut (or trivial), but accumulate and create severe agony over time. Trauma occurs if your nervous system is overwhelmed and your tolerance for painful feelings is exceeded. Trauma manifests differently in each individual. As a result, comparing trauma is a pointless exercise. Trauma can affect your attachment styles, resulting in what is referred to as "attachment trauma."

As you grow older, you develop two distinct attachment styles: insecure and secure. Insecurity manifests itself as inconsistency and injustice. Secure is a term that refers to constant emotional support. According to Dr. Bruce Perry, you may occasionally encounter patternless caregiving or care that combines support and neglect.

According to Very Well Mind, "neuroplasticity allows the brain to adapt to a person's changing behavioral habits and beliefs." Individuals who are insecurely attached can develop the necessary security by incorporating new, helpful, and loving experiences into their lives."

Discovering Your Inner Child and Creating a Healthy Connection

According to *Healthline*, the first step in healing is just acknowledging your inner child, which is "a process of self-discovery."

With self-compassion, embrace the inner child mindfully. Simply put, mindfulness is being present and in tune with oneself. Assemble with your inner child. Avoid passing judgment on your thoughts; instead, observe them objectively and express gratitude for their existence. Allow them their place. Your inner child suppressed things out of fear of taking up space. It's time to vent your anguish. It's time to recover your youth. It's time to restart.

When you show yourself compassion, some backdrafts may surface. On the path to healing, repressed pain may surface. If it becomes excessive, try grounding. Concentrate on your senses to bring yourself into the present moment. In this manner, your inner child won't take complete control without your approval.

Reconnect with Your Inner Child

Observe and then nurture your inner kid. Numerous exercises are included in Dr. Stefanie Stahl's book *The Child in You: The Breakthrough Method for Uncovering Your True Self.* Consider the following memory exercise: Take note of how you handled recent events in your life, such as unhealthy behaviors or negative thoughts. Then, consider what self-defense mechanisms can be detected in your behavior? Connect these to the beliefs you learned as a youngster that affect them.

Could you take note of it to alter it? Determine which of your negative beliefs result from conditioning and childhood training. Through your inner adult, reshape reality.

According to Dr. Stephanie Stahl, you can improve your inner adult by challenging childhood ideas formed due to neglect or abuse. Confront negative beliefs like "I don't deserve love because my parents didn't show it to me" with the affirmation" "I was just a child who deserved love and protection and still does."

Beginning the Process of Self-Repair

Here are some starters for addressing your inner child:

- What are some things you wish a trusted adult would have told you at that age?
- What is a complimentary statement you can make about yourself?
- How can you forgive yourself for not knowing what you know now when you were younger?
- How can you overcome the humiliation associated with your ordeal?

- What can you learn about wisdom from your wounded inner child?

Affirmations like "I love you" and "I'm sorry that happened" are *always* beneficial.

Release Oxytocin

Oxytocin is a hormone released when a person experiences feelings of love and security. It has several benefits, including stress alleviation, increased immunity, enhanced sleep, relaxation, and positive thinking. When a caregiver neglects a child, the release of oxytocin and other chemicals such as dopamine may be inhibited.

According to the study *Oxytocin's Effects on Maternal Care and Closeness*, "Oxytocin is created in the hypothalamus and released into the circulatory system, where it aids in uterine contractions during parturition and milk ejection during breastfeeding. Oxytocin is also delivered directly into the brain, where it has been demonstrated to be crucial in the establishment and maintenance of attachment bonds in animals."

The good news is that there are techniques to increase oxytocin levels in the brain. There are even studies investigating the use of oxytocin to induce feelings of trust and safety in children who have been deprived in some way.

As an adult, you can release oxytocin in the following ways to deal with your inner child:

1. Massage yourself or another person.
2. Yoga—helps to lower blood pressure and alleviates stress.
3. Bath—Soak in warm water with bubbles and let your mind wander away.

4. Weighted Blanket—It will feel like you're being hugged!
5. Listen to or create music for self-care.
6. Meditation—A timeless panacea!
7. Promote connection—A strong support system and social activities will aid in your recovery.
8. Intimacy—Hugs, cuddles, intercourse, or other physical contact with another person.
9. Domesticated animals—Emotional support animals have a good cause for their existence. Even if you don't have access to a pet, you can still benefit from the company of one.

Eventually, you'll accept your inner kid as an integral part of yourself. You'll know that nothing was your fault. You have to exist through white-knuckling and other forms of self-sufficiency. However, you can now allow it to seek refuge. Healing doesn't occur overnight. It's natural to have to review certain issues from time to time. You can work on it in segments. You aren't required to work through all of your early trauma in one sitting. However, your inner child will appreciate you for finally bringing it to the surface.

QUIZ ON FORGIVENESS

Are you a forgiving person? When someone wrongs you, are you more likely to turn a blind eye, slash their tires, or both?

The quiz below is based on a scale developed by forgiveness pioneer Michael McCullough and his colleagues, and it provides insight into our responses to those who wrong us.

Before you begin the quiz, consider someone who has wronged you—a friend, a spouse, a family member, or a coworker. Then, keeping that individual in mind, respond honestly to the following twelve questions, saying how much you agree or disagree with each statement.

The quiz will function like a mirror and when you're finished, you'll discover what it indicates about your typical response to being treated unfairly.

Take The Quiz

1. I'm going to make him/her pay.

- Strongly Disagree
- Disagree
- Neutral
- Agree
- Strongly Agree

2. I maintain a safe distance between us.

- Strongly Disagree
- Disagree
- Neutral
- Agree
- Strongly Agree

3. I want him/her to suffer some sort of misfortune.

- Strongly Disagree
- Disagree
- Neutral
- Agree
- Strongly Agree

4. I conduct my life as if he/she doesn't exist or isn't present.

- Strongly Disagree
- Disagree
- Neutral
- Agree
- Strongly Agree

5. I wholeheartedly agree.

- Strongly Disagree
- Disagree
- Neutral
- Agree
- Strongly Agree

6. I want him/her to receive what is due to him/her.

- Strongly Disagree
- Disagree
- Neutral
- Agree
- Strongly Agree

7. It's difficult for me to be warm toward him/her.

- Strongly Disagree
- Disagree
- Neutral
- Agree
- Strongly Agree

8. I avoid him/her.

- Strongly Disagree
- Disagree
- Neutral
- Agree
- Strongly Agree

9. I'm going to avenge myself.

- Strongly Disagree
- Disagree

- Neutral
- Agree
- Strongly Agree

10. I severed ties with him/her.
- Strongly Disagree
- Disagree
- Neutral
- Agree
- Strongly Agree

11. I desire to see him/her in pain and misery.
- Strongly Disagree
- Disagree
- Neutral
- Agree
- Strongly Agree

12. I distance myself from him/her.
- Strongly Disagree
- Disagree
- Neutral
- Agree
- Strongly Agree

Conclusion

If you enjoyed this title and would like to read about other topics that have changed my life, please check out my new books on Amazon or my website: www.my-mindguide.com.

Also, let's stay connected on social media. Please drop a line on Facebook or Instagram, and stay tuned for updates! You're welcome to share your thoughts with me directly as well: gassner@my-mindguide.com. In return, I'll send you a gorgeous infographic that you can cut out and frame.

Also, please leave a review on Amazon, as this will help me to reach an even broader audience. Thank you so much for your time, insight, and undying hunger for knowledge!

I want to say thank you to my beloved wife, Anneliese, who is always patient and has an open ear for my crazy ideas. Thank you to all of my colleagues, clients, friends, and family members, who have all contributed to what I am now.

I also want to say thank you to Gabriel Palacios, the king of hypnotherapy and a Swiss bestselling author who taught this old fox new tricks, letting me deep-dive into the mystery of hypnotherapy. I learned so much along the journey that I'm now a certified master-hypnosis coach and conversation coach myself!

Furthermore, I want to say thank you to the fantastic teachers of SAMYANA/Bali who trained me to become a certified yoga and meditation teacher.

Last but not least, I give a special thanks to my master-teacher Eckhard Wunderle, who's close to a saint to me. He introduced me to the world of meditation and let me discover all the wonders it has to offer. I couldn't be prouder about having received my certification as a meditation teacher directly from him at the Institut für Spirituelle Psychologie.

Peace, love, and happiness to all of you—till next time!

Authors Bio

Kurt Friedrich Gassner has worn many hats throughout his lifetime, including but not limited to serial entrepreneur, creative director, meditation teacher, licensed hypnotherapist, and more recently, self-improvement author. Leveraging his treasure trove of experiences and in-depth knowledge of psychology, he provides his readers with the tools they need to unlock their infinite potential.

As a prolific self-help writer, Kurt has authored the following books: *The Art of Forgiveness*, *Lie or Die*, *Soul-Match*, *Can You Inherit a Poisoned Mind?* and *The Power of Poverty*. He also authored a best-selling children's book in German-speaking countries and has over twenty books underway.

When it comes to enduring success, Kurt understands that financial prosperity isn't the only aspect one should strive for. He may be a self-made millionaire, but what really transformed his life is mastering his unconscious mind. Perseverance, personal power, self-awareness, and learning from past mistakes have all been key ingredients to bringing his dreams to fruition—and he strives to impart that wisdom to others through his writing.

In his spare time, Kurt Friedrich Gassner is either traveling across the globe, golfing, biking in the Alps, hiking, or spending quality time with his loved ones. For the last thirty-seven years, he has been happily married and he is the father of two successful children. Presently, he resides in both Munich, Germany, and Kirchberg, Austria.

UPCOMING BOOKS BY THE AUTHOR

Made in the USA
Middletown, DE
02 June 2022

66565232R00104